sucking the marrow out of life
the JOHN MACLEAN story
with paul connolly

sucking the marrow out of life
the JOHN MACLEAN story
with paul connolly

PIER
9

TO ALL MY FAMILY IN AUSTRALIA, CANADA AND SCOTLAND: MY FATHER, ALEX; MY MOTHER, ANNE; AND MY SIBLINGS, MARC, MARION, DON, MORAG AND KENNY. AND, OF COURSE, TO MY BIRTH MOTHER, AVRIL. I NEVER REALLY KNEW YOU BUT YOU INDELIBLY TOUCHED MY SOUL.

AT THE FINISH LINE OF THE NEPEAN TRIATHLON, 1994

LIST OF PHOTOGRAPHS

PROLOGUE

MY FATHER TELLS ME MY FIRST WORDS after the accident were 'How is my bike?' but I don't remember this. In fact, I recall virtually nothing of those first few days as I slipped in and out of consciousness. Memories of that time come to me only in ragged fragments, like scraps of paper torn from a much larger page.

I do recall seeing the white uniform of a nurse looming over me. I have vague memories of the whump of helicopter blades as I was transferred a few days after the accident from Sydney's Westmead Hospital to the Royal North Shore Hospital. And at some point, during a window of lucidity that closed almost as soon as it opened, I remember telling myself not to die; that as tempting as it would be to just close my eyes and give in, thereby escaping the extraordinary pain, I wasn't ready for that yet.

Not that you should mistake this for bravery or even heroism. It was simply instinct kicking in. I don't feel I'm different from anyone else. Not then, not now. Just like the wolf that will chew its own leg off to escape the killer jaws of a trap, we all want to live. Sometimes you don't know how much until the door to death is swung wide open and you find yourself clawing desperately at the door jamb with what feels like someone's boot in your back.

While there's much I don't remember, I do recall waking up after the accident in Royal North Shore's intensive care unit. I was a mess of wires and tubes and broken pieces, though exactly how many pieces I didn't know at the time. A buzzer lay near my left hand. And although pain seemed to be coming at me from every point on my body, I remember being immediately concerned about my legs. From my prone position, I couldn't see them. More worrying still, I couldn't feel them. I was sure they were gone.

It's impossible for me to overstate the importance I placed on my ability to run. For reasons I would only come to understand much later, my whole identity and self-esteem were tied up in it. I felt life was at its best when I was running as fast as I could. The fact that I was often running away from life is a paradox I appreciate only now, but back then, my legs were everything. They *had* to be there.

With panic rising, I pressed the buzzer with my left thumb, one of my few body parts that was actually working. The nurse can't have taken more than 30 seconds to respond, but it felt like an age.

'Where are my legs?' I asked her as she entered the room. 'Where are my legs, I can't feel them, have they been amputated?'

'They're here John, they're here,' she said, as, one at a time, she lifted them up for me to see.

Relief washed over me and, to celebrate, I promptly passed out.

01 MAHOGANY OR PINE

THERE WERE NO PORTENTS OR OMENS to suggest that 27 June 1988 would be an especially momentous day in my life. I didn't wake up with a funny feeling in my gut, the clouds didn't gather ominously on the horizon and, as far as I can recall, no black cats crossed my path.

In other words, I didn't see it coming. Welcome to Life, I guess.

What I do recall of that day is a general feeling of contentment. Though it wasn't something I was consciously aware of at the time, I was revelling in my youth, health and, especially, freedom. Less than a month earlier— just a few days after my 22nd birthday on 27 May—I'd moved out of the family home in Tregear, in western Sydney, and into my mate Michael Winter's place. Michael lived in the quiet Blue Mountains town of Faulconbridge, some 30 kilometres west of Tregear and about 75 kilometres west of Sydney.

It was liberating to strike out on my own and I'd found a perfect housemate in Michael who, somewhat surprisingly given that he was about the same age as me, was a fastidious cleaner and a creative cook. (As luck would have it, these were not my strong points so, from my point of view at least, Michael and I complemented each other nicely. Michael, I'm sure, would have a different take on it.)

If it was liberating for me, it was also a release for my father, Alex. You often hear of parents struggling to deal with their children leaving the family nest but, if I recall correctly, Dad wasn't exactly in turmoil when I told him of my intention to move in with Michael, with whom I played semi-professional rugby league. 'I'll help you pack the truck,' Dad said, before the words were out of my mouth. 'Anytime you like. Just ask.'

Kind of chokes you up, doesn't it?

I remember that 27 June was a Monday and I had a rostered day off from my job as a groundsman and odd-job man at a local primary school. I had recently discovered the relatively new sport of triathlon and I had enough appreciation of the mix of disciplines (swimming, cycling and running over varying distances) to have completed two triathlons in my local area. But my main interest in it was that it would provide ideal cross-training for rugby league, the tough 13-a-side form of football developed in working-class northern England a century ago and taken up with gusto soon after by Australia's eastern states. In the realisation of a childhood dream, I'd been earning a wage playing the game for a few years and, all going well, hoped to continue doing so for some time.

So that particular Monday—a day after I'd put in a starring performance for Warragamba Rugby League Club in the Group 6 country competition—I decided on a long bike ride. My chosen route would take me from Faulconbridge, eastwards down the snaking mountain highway and across the vast Nepean River valley to the Penrith suburb of St Clair. Then I'd turn around and come back; a round trip of some 80 kilometres.

Part of the reason my trip would take in St Clair was that I planned to drop in on a mate who was building a tandem bicycle for me. My aim was to recruit another friend, Colin Thomas, so that he and I could have a crack at reaching 100 kilometres per hour while cycling down the mountains on the highway. I'd often managed to reach an eye-bulging 82 kilometres per hour

A PICTURE OF THE SEEMING INVINCIBILITY OF YOUTH: AGED 20, ON HAWAII'S WAIKIKI BEACH DURING AN
END-OF-SEASON FOOTBALL TRIP IN 1986

on my own, but I figured that on a tandem bike, with an extra set of legs in front of me, I could crack three figures. Admittedly, it wasn't exactly one of humankind's most profound challenges but it greatly appealed to the boy in me, who even now, at 39, makes himself known regularly.

Around midday I was on my way back home, happy in the knowledge that the tandem was coming together nicely. The cycle to St Clair, performed with Talking Heads pumping through my headphones, had been, in part, an exhilarating downhill rush. But ahead of me, on the return leg, was a long punishing hill and I knew my lungs and legs would soon be aching and my heart pounding as the gradient increased. In a masochistic way I looked forward to it—not to the pain but to the challenge, or at least the conquering of the challenge and the associated feelings afterwards.

Leaving St Clair, I wound my way through the kind of unremarkable suburban back streets that I'd grown up around. I soon entered the on-ramp for the M4 motorway, then a dual-carriageway, four-lane road with a wide enough shoulder for bicycles, though there were never too many of them about. I stood up on my pedals, pushed hard to gather momentum, and did my best to keep a smooth line while avoiding the rocks, glass and other debris that finds itself pushed to the margins of roadways.

And it's at this point that my recollections of that day become unreliable. It's odd to think that what I do seem to remember may actually be counterfeit: pictures in my mind pieced together from eyewitness reports and police and ambulance paperwork and photographs. All I know for sure is that at about 12.30pm, my legs were pumping, the sky was a brilliant blue and I was racing home, when a white, eight-ton Mitsubishi Pantec truck hit me from behind at about 110 kilometres per hour and changed the course of my life forever.

WHEN PEOPLE SUCCUMB TO THEIR INEVITABLE CURIOSITY and ask me about the various injuries and scars that remain from the accident, particularly an obvious pencil-long gash along the edge of my right bicep, I do occasionally have a bit of fun with them. 'Back in my young days, before the accident, I used to be a bit of a hood,' I tell them in as serious a voice as I can manage. 'This one here on my bicep is the result of a knife fight outside a nightclub. It was pretty gruesome at the time but you should see what happened to the other bloke.'

The cause of my injuries, of course, the reason I ended up where I am today, is, by comparison, so banal. But in a way, that's what makes it all the more frightening, as it underlines the fragility and randomness of life. You don't need to be doing anything wrong for everything as you know it to be turned on its head. Sometimes you just need to be in the wrong place at the wrong time.

So it happened like this. A truck driver, looking to overtake a vehicle ahead, attempts to change lanes on a long, straight, unremarkable stretch of road. As he glances in his right-side mirror to make sure the coast is clear, his truck drifts to the left. Imperceptible to the driver, but exactly far enough to ram the cyclist—that'd be me—who is, by comparison, crawling along between the boundary of the left lane and a corrugated-iron guard rail that glints like a blade. The impact is hard enough to break both the truck's left indicator light and headlight, but the driver doesn't even notice and motors ahead. Finally, about a kilometre down the road, he's pulled up by a motorcyclist who was following him and saw the whole thing happen.

The sun was still shining and the world was still spinning when I was catapulted end over end through the air. I'm sure I was already unconscious when I bounced and skidded for metres along the bitumen, before finally careering into the guard rail and coming to rest.

A teenager called Michael McKenzie, whom I would meet many years afterwards, saw it all unfold from the backseat of his mother's car, which was travelling in the opposite direction. He was staring idly out of the window when he saw the truck crash into me, just near the Kingswood Road overpass, and he screamed out to her to stop. By the time she did, and by the time this young boy ran across the road to see if I was okay, there was already a priest on hand giving me the last rites. (As fate would have it, the priest had been travelling some way behind the truck and was one of the first at my side.)

Arriving soon after were the Penrith forensic police, who had been called to the area with the news that a cyclist was dead, though I wasn't quite that. Their quick arrival accounts for photographs taken of me at the scene which, for a long time, were difficult for me to look at.

Anyway, before long I was in the back of an ambulance as they raced me to Westmead Hospital, about 40 kilometres away. I dare say the sirens were blaring, but the paramedics must have wondered if there was any point in rushing—I can't imagine they held out much hope for me. I was a mess.

When I was admitted to hospital that afternoon, my list of injuries took emergency doctors on a thorough tour of my body. Westmead's admission diagnosis makes note of 'pulmonary contusion, retroperitoneal haemorrhage, head trauma, chest trauma, vertebral trauma, pelvic trauma, extremity fractures, bacterial pneumonia ...' The list goes on. In plainer English, I had broken my back in three places, my pelvis in four places and my right arm in two places. I had two fractures in my sternum, broken ribs, both my lungs were punctured (which accounted for the speedy onset of pneumonia) and I required seven units (about 3 litres) of blood. My right knee was ripped off the bone and I had countless lacerations and road rash—the result of skin meeting the unforgiving hardness of road, gravel and concrete—from head to toe.

Dad was the first to be contacted after the accident and he notified my elder siblings, Marc and Marion, and my girlfriend, Michelle. As sometimes happens in the frantic aftermath of an emergency, the full seriousness of my injuries did not immediately filter through to Dad and the others. At first, everyone thought I had sustained a broken pelvis but was not in any immediate danger. For this reason Dad was somewhat surprised at being shut out of the emergency room for many hours. It was only when a surgeon came to see him that he discovered the full extent of the damage I'd sustained. Dad was told to prepare himself: I was not expected to live.

A few years ago, I came across a male nurse who was working at Westmead Hospital at the time I was brought in after the accident. He illustrated starkly just how dire the outlook was and, while he was at it, gave an insight into the black humour needed in hospitals to ensure the staff's sanity in a frequently distressing environment. He told me how the talk among some of the emergency operating team was whether I'd prefer mahogany or pine. For my coffin, that is.

Thankfully, it's not a choice my family had to make, though to be honest, it would have been easy. Pine. After all, I was from Tregear, a working-class suburb of working-class Mt Druitt, deep in the heart of working-class western Sydney. My family could never have afforded mahogany.

AFTER FOUR DAYS DRIFTING IN AND OUT OF CONSCIOUSNESS, I woke up. If Dad remembers my first words being an enquiry about the condition of my bike, Mum recalls me asking her if I was ever going to run again, which, she says, cut her to the quick and elicited a flood of tears and a hasty retreat from my bedside. But whatever I said first hardly matters, I suppose. The point is, I was alive.

Most instrumental to my survival was, undoubtedly, the work of medical staff at the scene of the accident and at Westmead and Royal North Shore hospitals. Without their efforts my life would have ended back in 1988 when I was 22, barely a man. For that I'll always be grateful, and it amazes me to think that in a few years' time I'll have lived more of my life post-accident than I had pre-accident.

I also believe that my survival chances—as well as my ability to cope with what happened to me—were aided by the strength of my body, honed by years of training and vigorous contact sport. Mentally, too, I was used to taking knocks and getting up after them, and to playing on despite feeling the worse for wear. Of course, getting smashed by a truck is considerably more distressing than getting pummelled by a 100-kilogram rugby league prop, but I can't help but feel that my life in sport prepared me, in some small way, for the fight ahead. And then, as I've said, there was my raw, primal, stubborn human will to live. Under any circumstances. No matter how distressing and life changing they might be.

Which brings me back to my legs, lying there immobile beneath those starchy white hospital sheets all those years ago.

Oddly enough, I can't ever remember a time in those early days when I had The Conversation. You know, the one delivered in grave tones by a senior member of medical staff that goes something like, 'John, as you know, you've been in a shocking accident. I'm so sorry to tell you that due to the injuries you sustained to your back and spinal cord, in all likelihood you will never walk again.'

I'm sure if I had been on the receiving end of such news I wouldn't have forgotten it, although I guess there is the chance that I *was* told and immediately erased the conversation from my memory bank, because at the time it would have been just about the worst news I could have heard.

In any case, I simply can't remember being informed. Perhaps everyone assumed someone else had told me. Or perhaps no one felt the need to tell me because, well, it was all pretty obvious. I couldn't move my legs and after leaving intensive care I was placed in a spinal ward, surrounded by men being pushed about in wheelchairs, or worse, confined, completely immobile, to bed. Clearly there was something seriously wrong with me.

Yet I remained stubbornly positive. Because of the imprecise nature of my spinal injury, I never quite accepted at the time that I was a paraplegic and would never walk, let alone run, again. And I was all too ready to accept any information that confirmed my optimism.

On one occasion I was visited by my elder brother Marc, whose words of hope came in the form of an analogy I could relate to. 'John, you've had a serious accident but I want you to think of your recovery as a race,' Marc said. 'You've had many races over the years but this will be a marathon, not a sprint. But you'll get to the finish line in the end, don't worry.'

Some time later I remember welcoming Dr Atif Gabrael to my bedside. A father figure to me, Dr Gabrael was also my family doctor, and he'd been patching me up and putting me back together for as long as I could remember. I guess you could say he knew me inside and out. 'Don't worry, John,' he told me, in his warm, reassuring tones, 'one day you'll be bigger, stronger and faster than ever before.' Who was I, a groundsman with a poor academic record, to argue with a trained medical practitioner? His words gave me considerable strength and hope.

Dr Gabrael wasn't just trying to console me with a lie, although he told me many years later that he was too distressed by the accident and what it had done to me to convey anything but hope ('For without hope, John, what have we got? Why would we get out of bed every day?'). There actually *was* a slim chance that I would walk again. All spinal injuries are different, with much of their impact dictated by where and to what extent the spinal cord is damaged. My spinal cord was damaged at T12, at about the level of the navel, but it wasn't severed. This made me, to use the correct terminology, 'incomplete'. As time has shown, it's been both a blessing and a curse. While my specific case of incompleteness allows me some feeling in my legs, particularly my left, it's not enough to walk. The messages from my brain don't get through without interruption, and my leg muscles are wasted. Nevertheless, for brief painful periods, I can stand on my left leg aided by Canadian crutches (which support the forearm rather than prop the armpits). I am very fortunate to be able to do this for it allows me a broader range of access than if I were completely restricted to a wheelchair.

On the downside, the specifics of my injury mean I am hypersensitive to long periods of pressure. If I sit down too long (and I can't sit on anything but cushioned surfaces) the pain in my backside is considerable and there's a danger of developing pressure sores. And once you get them, they take a long time to go away. I can stand up to relieve the pain momentarily but that brings its own discomfort after a minute or two. So I can't sit for too long and I can't stand for too long. Which all means that whenever I can, I try to lie down and get on my back. Better still, I go to sleep. Only then am I completely, blissfully, free from pain.

But I'm getting ahead of myself.

All this I'd discover later. First, I had to heal.

A FORENSIC POLICE PHOTOGRAPH TAKEN NEAR THE SCENE OF THE ACCIDENT SHOWS THAT WHILE IT
COMPLETELY CHANGED THE COURSE OF MY LIFE, THE TRUCK THAT RAN ME DOWN SUSTAINED ONLY
SUPERFICIAL DAMAGE TO ITS LEFT HEADLIGHT AND INDICATOR

GET ME OUT OF HERE

02 GET ME OUT OF HERE

AS IT TURNED OUT, I'D BROKEN FIFTEEN BONES, which was a record for the spinal ward. I've always been a competitive bloke, but I couldn't quite enjoy the glory of this achievement due to the constant agony I was in. If Westmead Hospital was about a fight to survive, Royal North Shore Hospital was about enduring pain like I'd never known before. All I could think about was the pain and, more to the point, escaping it.

Painkillers were, of course, a blessing, but they could only mute the agony, not eliminate it altogether. Every couple of hours—and once a day when the sheets were changed—I would have to be lifted by four orderlies and flipped onto my side, or from my side onto my back, to help prevent pressure sores developing. This was complicated by the rawness of my shredded skin, which would stick to the sheets and be reopened every time I was lifted up, leaving behind a bloody imprint.

If I was in pain, so were my family and friends. The effects of an accident like mine radiate like shockwaves through so many lives. Family, friends, teammates, employers, workmates and acquaintances were all touched by what happened to me and I was never short of visitors. My family was a constant presence: my father Alex, my (step)mother Anne, my brother and idol, Marc, and my sister Marion. Though I didn't know it then, my accident would prove a catalyst for much introspection, re-evaluation and change in my life, mostly for the better. Contrary to all expectations, bad can beget good. I've seen it first-hand too many times to doubt it.

One of the major changes in my life sparked by the accident was the growth in my relationship with my siblings. Up until then, to put it simply, I was the annoying shadow who followed Marc about, admiring him and hoping to steal, as if by osmosis, some of his abundant talents as an athlete and student. To Marion, two years my senior, I was either invisible or a constant source of irritation. But my accident forced us to consider each other in new ways—as real, independent and ultimately fragile people rather than as mere extras in our respective life dramas. As a result, my accident would deepen my relationship with both Marion and Marc. Perhaps that would have happened anyway, with age and maturity. But perhaps it wouldn't have.

Of all my visitors, the most regular was undoubtedly my girlfriend, Michelle. Every single day for four months, even on days when she had worked a full shift as a secretary, Michelle drove from her office in western Sydney to Royal North Shore to see me, a round trip of about three hours conducted through peak-hour traffic. Most people would have been too exhausted and frayed by such a long day to offer anything but cursory comfort on arrival, but Michelle never seemed less than fully charged. It was obvious that she would do anything for me and, as such, she was an incredible source of strength and support.

Ironically, however, Michelle, perhaps more than anyone else, reminded me (inadvertently, I should make clear) of the possible consequence of my injuries, something which, for the most part, I successfully denied to myself. Seeing her so frequently made me wonder how it would affect our relationship if I was, in fact, restricted to a wheelchair for the rest of my life. She was only 22, and it seemed completely unfair that her life would be potentially limited through no fault of her own. So, during one of her visits, I remember saying to her, quite calmly, that we should call it a day. 'You should leave me and meet someone else,' I said, barely able to look at her, focusing instead on the window and the magnificent view it afforded of the brick wall of an adjoining building. 'You should meet someone else. Someone you can walk along the beach with.'

That simple pleasure, I felt then, was quite possibly lost to me and, by association, Michelle. How could I deny her the freedom to take her partner by the hand and stroll along on the hard sand with the water lapping around her feet? I wouldn't have wanted to be denied the freedom to do that with a partner and I didn't feel Michelle should have to be either.

As I would discover later, her family told her the same thing and I respect them for saying that. They wanted the best for their daughter. I was convinced in my mind that I couldn't give Michelle the life I thought she should have. They must have felt the same.

But Michelle, to her credit, wasn't going anywhere and I'll always love her for that. 'Don't be silly, John, I want to stay with you. I want to stay with *you*,' she said, tears running down her cheeks. 'What's happened doesn't make any difference to me.'

Back then I had no inkling of what love was about. To me, it had a lot to do with sex and having someone to hang around with on weekends. Considering that, it's little wonder that, prior to Michelle, none of my previous relationships had reached any great heights. I think it's fair to say that at the time of my accident I was an emotionally stunted human being. So I could 'see' in my head the significance of Michelle's answer but I couldn't actually feel it.

This lack of emotional maturity affected me on more than a romantic level. It was a much broader malaise that affected not only my relationships with other people but also my understanding of myself. It meant that while, from time to time, I allowed myself a brief private cry at the state I was in, I never explored the furthest reaches of my soul to see how it had been affected by the accident. That would have been a perfectly normal and even healthy thing to do, I realise now; but, incredibly, I didn't do it, despite the support offered by a lovely hospital psychologist called Helen. As a result, for a very long time I didn't even begin to process my grief.

I think that mostly had to do with the fact that I didn't know how one went about such things. The language I'd grown up with, the language my family spoke, was not emotionally articulate. Feelings, desires, fears, even joy, were not things we were ever encouraged to speak about. Nor were tears indulged. If something bad happened to you, according to Dad's pared-down strategy for dealing with the world, you just had to be a 'tough little soldier' and get on with it. It was as simple, and as difficult, as that.

But practice makes perfect, and by the time I had my accident I could safely skim the surface of my emotions and get by just fine, thank you very much. The blackness beneath, with all its slimy weeds and slippery stones, was a place I wouldn't fully immerse myself in for another fifteen years.

WHILE MY INABILITY TO GO WITHIN MYSELF and grieve deeply for what had happened left me emotionally deficient, it had plenty of benefits that made a huge difference to my recovery. I can't deny this. For one thing, it allowed me almost immediately to see the positives in my situation, and I clung to them like a man clings to a piece of driftwood after his ship has gone down.

Yes, my enjoyment of life up to this point had centred on my natural affinity—an affinity I happily honed with hours of practice and training—for running and all forms of athletic endeavour. And, yes, I was actually making something of a living playing rugby league, as I'd always dreamed I would. So to feel that that had suddenly been taken away from me was a bitter pill to swallow. But at the same time, I was alive. When that truck hit me a coin was tossed in the air and it came down in my favour. I was alive.

I understand that some medical staff at Royal North Shore had made a note to keep an eye on me, fearing that when my recovery got to the point where I had a certain level of independence, I might attempt to kill myself. They knew my situation, the value I placed on my legs, and figured it could drive me to the edge, the black precipice. They'd seen it happen before:

men and women, unable to cope with the magnitude of their loss, who took their own lives, sometimes by pulling themselves up and over an upper-storey hospital balcony.

But I never got close to that. Despite defining myself so strongly in terms of my physicality, I never once wished I was dead. I think coming so close to death actually made me realise more than ever how strongly I valued life.

Nor did it hurt that the day I was transferred from the intensive care unit and placed in the spinal ward, I found myself sharing a room with three other men, all quadriplegics, paralysed from the neck down. Even as physically ruined as I was, how could I—who still held on to the faint hope I'd be fully restored, but at the worst would be left a paraplegic—complain about my predicament when there were others much worse off than me? It was an immediate lesson in humility and it's one I often contemplate when I find the going tough in life. There's always someone worse off than you.

Having said all that, I loathed my time in hospital, and the harsh realities of healing and institutionalised care tested my positivity. First, there was the pain, which inevitably intensified when, after a month in the spinal ward, I told the medical staff to take me off the morphine. That happened the day a nurse informed me they wanted to slowly reduce my intake of painkillers. 'It's probably better to wean you off slowly,' he said. But I asked him to rip the IV drip out completely, and said that I was okay with that. So he did. This wasn't a decision I took lightly but, with my mind focused on healing, I didn't want to risk addiction to painkillers, if only because that would give me another hurdle to clear further down the track.

Part of me also wanted to face my pain head on, to take the full force of it. Only then would I know what I was dealing with and how to beat it. Perhaps it was just bravado, but I figured my background playing rugby league would help. As those who have played the game know, it's not for the faint of heart. With no substantial padding, you do your best to run around an opponent, but more times than not, you run head on into an opposition player who's intent on driving you into the ground to complete a tackle. You get used to playing injured and playing in pain. So they took me off painkillers and, well, it was a shock. An awful, face-slapping shock, but I'm glad I did it.

But there was more to deal with than just the pain. Due to the very nature of my injuries I had to forgo any sense of privacy. For instance, I loathed sponge baths. While the nurses were always totally professional, I couldn't help but hate the predicament I was in. Just weeks earlier I'd been a fit, healthy, strong, independent 22-year-old, and now here I was, so helpless I couldn't wash myself. It was as if someone had said to me on admission, 'Leave your dignity at the door, Mr Maclean. You can pick it up on your way out.'

It got worse. While the catheter—an uncomfortable piece of equipment, I can tell you—took care of my bladder, I also had to be given daily enemas. With no feeling below my waist, the communication lines were down between my brain and my waste-management system, so the catheter and nurse-assisted enemas were a necessary, though intensely humiliating, part of my daily ritual. This was a window into a possible future and it filled me with dread. Could I cope, I asked myself, with living in adult diapers, the strict bathroom regimens, and whatever else it would take to manage my lack of function in this area?

In addition, there were countless routines and rules that compounded my frustration. I'd be given needles to stop my blood clotting; I'd wear stockings to prevent deep-vein thrombosis; I'd have my hair cut when someone who was not me decided I needed my hair cut; and I'd be constantly flipped in my bed, like a steak on a barbecue. And each time, my skin would rupture, my body would scream out and another little part of my spirit would be diminished.

In so many ways I felt like a candle burnt down to the wick. I was that low in spirit.

DURING THIS TIME I WAS STILL RECEIVING VISITORS and they invariably helped to lift my spirits, however momentarily, however unconventionally. I recall Colin Thomas (the long-time footballing friend who was set to join me for the tandem bicycle downhill speed record) coming in to see me one day early on. I'm not sure what he was expecting to see but it wasn't what he found. Shocked and overcome by emotion, poor Colin could only retreat as far as a bedside curtain before throwing up, making an enemy of the ward nurse who made him clean it up himself.

About a month later, Colin returned with another friend, Warren Hurst. They'd both ridden their bicycles all the way from Lethbridge Park, which was near Tregear; a 50-kilometre one-way trip that included a hair-raising cycle across the Sydney Harbour Bridge. Just prior to their visit I'd finally convinced a nurse, after much pleading, to make me a big bowl of salad out of all the fruit I'd been given by visitors. She was putting the final touches to my wish when Hursty and Colin arrived, so, to save a trip to my room, she handed them the brimming bowl and asked them to pass it on to me.

Without a word, the sweaty pair entered my room and proceeded to eat the fruit salad in front of me. Nothing I said slowed their progress and, with some dismay, I could see the level of fruit getting lower and lower. Surely they would leave me something? Not a scrap. Eventually they were done and the bowl was put down on my side-table, making a distinctly hollow sound. They then turned around, bent forward, dropped their Lycra cycling shorts and flashed their arses at me. 'We gotta get back,' they said—the only words to leave their mouths during the duration of their visit.

Hursty and Colin thought their prank was hilarious, and I probably would have done the same thing to them had our situations been reversed. In a weird way, it was an expression of love and a much-needed dose of normality.

It was also lovely to be visited by the principal and teachers from Bennett Road Public School, where I worked. Not only did they bring their own well wishes but they also passed on brightly coloured cards made for me by the schoolchildren. Invariably the kids addressed me as 'Mr John', since that's what they used to call me when they saw me riding my bike to school, or when I played handball with them in the playground at lunchtime. I was very touched by the gesture.

Out of all my visitors, I remember one more because of how our friendship would develop than because of anything he said or did at the time.

John Young, or 'Johnno', was a teammate of mine at Warragamba. He was the team's prop, a no-nonsense position for a no-nonsense bloke, as I quickly discovered. He weighed 115 kilograms, stood 192 centimetres tall and was a man's man. By this I mean that he didn't say too much about his emotions or express his feelings in any overt kind of way. A hand on the back from Johnno was as close as you'd get to a hug.

At the time of my accident, Johnno and I had played about a season and a half together, which is not really a lot. But every Sunday evening for four months, without fail, Johnno (most of the time accompanied by his girlfriend—and future wife—Gail) would stride into my room, ask me how I was going, and give me a commentary on the team's performance that day. When he ran out of things to talk about, Johnno would hang about silently, just being there. I can't adequately explain how that was abundantly sufficient for me, but it was.

Johnno, I could feel, was about to become a fixture in my life.

IN ALL, I SPENT ABOUT EIGHT WEEKS FLAT ON MY BACK, staring out of a window at bricks—and yes, I counted them, many times over—wondering when I'd ever see blue sky again, or hear a bird sing, or simply breathe fresh air. When you've got those things, I knew from experience, you barely notice them. When they're taken away, they seem like the whole world.

But there were a few high points, pricks of light in the gloom. Some time in the first month of my convalescence, for instance, I can recall being so sick of being on my back or my side that I turned myself over and lay on my stomach. It was an energy-sapping, painful struggle but the relief at being off my back and sides was blissful.

Of course, when the nurse came in and found me in such a position, she went crazy and scolded me as if I was a disobedient schoolboy. From her point of view, which was a good one, I'd risked further damaging my spine and knitting bones, just to flip myself. But it was worth the tongue lashing. Oh, the decadence of turning yourself over in bed. This is what my life had become.

Perhaps my fondest memory came about five weeks in, when I was told by a nurse that I could have a shower. Slowly and carefully, I was shifted from my bed and laid flat on an unadorned trolley. I was then wheeled into a large, bright shower recess.

Above me the shower head seemed full of promise. After the nurse adjusted the water temperature and directed the shower flow over me, I wasn't disappointed. After more than a month of bird baths, of the unavoidable harshness of sponge on torn skin, and of the pressure of mattress on my immobile limbs, the sensation of warm water falling on and washing over my skin was more than special. It was divine, and I all but wept with pleasure.

But hospital was an emotional rollercoaster and a major fall—a heart-in-the-mouth plummet, in fact—was just around the corner.

A few weeks on from that shower, I remember being positioned in bed above the horizontal for the first time. This had to be done ever so gradually, because when you're in the same position for such a long time the blood literally pools. As soon as my head came up off the pillow I had a feeling of vertigo, so it was a slow and steady process. I suppose it was like a deep-sea diver having to resurface gradually so as not to get 'the bends'. But eventually, although in considerable pain, I was sitting upright.

Over the following weeks the process was repeated to the point where I could sit myself up in bed and, eventually, with assistance, get myself into a wheelchair. Now I could be wheeled around the ward from time to time, if only to offer me brief changes of scenery. Finally, after slowly and methodically working up to it, I was able to get myself into a commode chair and take myself to the bathroom.

The first time this happened I wheeled past a mirror, the first one I'd seen since before the accident. Casually glancing over, I caught my reflection and did a double take. I didn't recognise the person looking back at me. It nearly made me physically ill to see myself. How I had changed in so short a time. How frighteningly fast my body had atrophied.

I was a shell of the person I had been just a few months earlier. I was drained of life. My muscles and tanned skin were replaced by bones and the ashen pallor of the dead. My normally sun-bleached hair was dark. I was covered in scars, and my eyes—as dull and impenetrable as those of a fish—were pushed back inside my skull. Seeing myself like this scared me no end.

Suddenly I knew what that look was on the faces of family and friends who had come to see me. This was what they saw. It was sickening to me. And in the darkness of that moment I believed I saw my true self for the first time. This was my core, I told myself. This was me with everything stripped away; my physical and material masks removed. No muscles, no fragrance, no fashionable clothes. It was humbling, confronting and shocking. It shook my resolve. In that moment I reached one of my lowest ebbs.

Just look at yourself, I said to the thing in the mirror. Look at you. What a wreck. Look at your withered legs. Look at your foul body. Who is going to ever be interested in you again? I can't even stand to look at you myself.

SOMEHOW THAT FEELING PASSED as I threw myself into my rehabilitation, determined to reclaim my old life and my old self. I suppose vanity played a small role in that. Of more influence, however, was my refusal to give in and give up hope. If there was a chance that I would walk again—however slim it might be—then that was good enough for me. I simply had to put myself in the best possible position to allow that to happen. Imploding in self-pity would not have helped.

Whatever the catalyst was, once I set myself that goal, my every waking thought was about turning back the clock to my life pre-accident. I simply longed to get out of hospital, and I wanted to run again. Not just walk, but run. I wanted the exact life I'd had before the truck hit me. I wanted to go back to playing football, I wanted my old job at the school, I wanted to reclaim my barely enjoyed freedom at Michael's house in Faulconbridge. Everything I'd had, I wanted to get back.

In a bold statement, I announced to Helen, the hospital psychologist, that when I finally left the hospital I would be walking out of there. Effectively, I took myself to the foot of Everest and dared myself to climb it.

So I ate as much as I could. I unflinchingly accepted all my injections, tablet cocktails and protein drinks. I warmly accepted the amazing help I was offered from doctors, physiotherapists, occupational therapists and anyone else assigned to aid me in my recovery. While I'm sure I wasn't Helen's greatest client (purely because, in so short a time, I couldn't suddenly learn how to tap into and articulate the contents of my heart), I was an eager physical patient. This was something I knew.

I had a lot of work ahead of me. For one thing, my right hand had suffered significant nerve damage in the accident. Using a special brace with tiny pulleys made from fishing line, I had to encourage the ulna nerve to re-connect, then teach it a full range of movement. This took some time.

Once my hand started to come good (and my right arm, which had been broken, pinned and plated, continued to heal), I had to pack muscle and strength back into my arms and torso. An easy way to do this was by pulling myself up into a seated position using a triangular bracket above the bed. Because my frame had withered considerably, this feat was still all but impossible in the early stages. It was also difficult on an emotional level because I felt it drew adverse attention to my relative 'health'. My roommates were all quadriplegics, and I could only imagine how envious they must have felt watching me. Perhaps this just reflected how envious I would have felt had I been in their position, for they never actually said anything to me.

Once I was able to leave my bed, I willingly endured the convoluted process (bed to sliding board, sliding board to wheelchair, wheelchair to plastic chair) that had to be undertaken to get me into the hydrotherapy pool in the bowels of the hospital. There, supported by inflated wine casks sewn into a cheesecloth sling, I learned how to swim all over again.

The plan was that gradually, over time, I would try to swim further and further, incrementally increasing my strength and stamina while the water, supporting me, made it easier. The pool was 25 metres long, but on that first day it looked as long and treacherous as the English Channel and I only managed to swim two strokes. Just two strokes. Racked with exhaustion, I was assisted from the pool, dried off and taken back to my room. I was asleep before my head hit the pillow.

I struggled similarly with my first few 'steps' on the parallel bars. Though it was more an exercise for my arms and shoulders, I learned to throw my legs in front of me, mimicking the art of walking.

While my physical therapy was initially painful and incredibly exhausting, it created a positive momentum because, little by little, I could see slight improvements in myself; not just in range of movement or strokes swum, or in my muscle tone, but gradually in my state of mind, too. Pushed and encouraged by the staff, I could feel myself getting stronger. And the stronger I grew, the more independent I became, now getting about in a wheelchair without assistance.

With my renewed strength came, thankfully, confirmation that I hadn't lost sexual function. Sexual impotency is one of the tragic consequences of many spinal injuries. To lose conventional sexual functionality must put an awful strain on one's sense of self and on one's relationships. I was incredibly lucky that this wasn't a problem I was forced to deal with.

My fears were allayed, some time into my recovery, when Michelle and I had what you could call a conjugal get-together in a private room attached to the hospital. Initially nervous and tentative, it was obviously a very different experience from usual in that my range of movement was limited, but I was happy to note that all monitored systems were functioning.

There was further good news (I don't mean to be crude, I just don't want to omit any of the realities of my situation) when one day, doing aided leg extensions, my bladder voided and I wet myself. Any embarrassment this caused me was far outweighed by the significance of the accident. Until then, every emptying of my bladder and bowels was a mechanical process. There were the enemas, and I had learned how to self-catheterise—to mechanically empty the contents of my bladder. If I hadn't done so, my bladder, which had forgotten how to function, would have remained full, causing headaches and increasing blood pressure, which in extreme cases can lead to death.

So on the day I wet myself, as odd as it sounds, I gave thanks. The episode of incontinence suggested that I was getting normal function back and that perhaps I wouldn't have to spend the rest of my life dealing with the debilitating, frustrating and inconvenient daily task of manually managing my waste, as I had feared. This was a huge development and I went back to my room, changed, got into my wheelchair and went straight down to the hospital chapel to say thanks.

While I was not, and am not, formally religious, I felt compelled, out of gratitude, to enter the chapel. I wonder if it was the influence of my brother, Marc, and others—who I was told were praying for me—that prompted me to do this. I'm not exactly sure, even now, but on that day I did have a sense of a bigger picture. I saw my fragility and insignificance; how, despite the walls we build up—walls suggesting we've got it together—we don't have all the answers; we don't have the absolute control over our lives that we sometimes think we do. Essentially, I'd been treated fortunately and I felt compelled to say thanks.

Thinking back on this now, I can see how I'd already begun to change—from the person my brother Marc recalls as a 'likeable larrikin', yet one who 'still had a long way to go as far as personal maturity was concerned'. Marc believes that prior to the accident I had the naive belief that everyone is basically good and life is a walk in the park. The accident, he says, was a harsh counter-argument to my fairly simple outlook on life.

When you're lying in a hospital bed you've got a lot of time to think. Perhaps I just hadn't had the opportunity before—when my days and thoughts were full of football, girls and cars—but in these early months after the accident, I slowly began the lifelong adventure of discovering just who I was and, just as significantly, who I was to become.

Being in that spinal ward started the process. I was learning and growing in new ways. Perhaps the accident stripped me of my ego—something reinforced by the shock I experienced at seeing myself in front of that mirror. And that left a void. Room, if I was smart and lucky enough, that I could fill with more vital and, ultimately, more meaningful qualities.

I KNEW MY TIME IN HOSPITAL WAS COMING TO A CLOSE when I was allowed to escape for a day and go out with Michelle and a small group of our friends to Centennial Park, a sprawling green lung east of Sydney's centre. Initially I felt fragile and incredibly vulnerable leaving the confines of the hospital, as if a breath of wind could knock me down and reintroduce the kind of pain I'd tried so hard to escape. But gradually that was forgotten, as the sunlight fell upon my skin for the first time in four months. There was a sense of being reborn, of seeing things as if for the first time. The trees, the fish in the pond, the fullness of life. It was an incredibly special day for me, topped off brilliantly by an ice-cream—rum and raisin, my perennial favourite—on the way back to the hospital.

My next half-day excursion from hospital was to Michelle's house. We had some friends around for a barbecue and if I recall rightly, her father cooked fish—snapper, I think it was. After four months of hospital fare, it was heavenly.

After those excursions I started to get out more in and around the hospital, even doing hill repeats in my day chair up a small incline in the hospital grounds. One day I would manage 12 metres. The next I'd try for 13 metres. And so on. The athlete in me was re-emerging.

And in the end, after four of the longest, most traumatic months of my life, I did what I said I'd do and walked out of hospital. Well, sort of. In front of my father and Helen, I pushed my wheelchair from my room to the elevator. Using all my strength and the small amount of feeling in my left leg, I lifted myself up and stood, assisted by crutches. And I stood all the way from the seventh floor down to the hospital foyer. From there I walked, in a fashion, taking almost all the weight on my crutches (and what weight I could on my left leg while propping on my useless right leg), across the lobby, past admissions and through the automatic doors. There I negotiated a slight rise up to the car park before sitting back down in my wheelchair in preparation for the car ride home.

So I climbed that Everest after all and my journey back to my old life, I believed, was well under way.

03 BEGINNINGS

BEFORE GOING FORWARD, I should probably go back and say what I need to say about my childhood. They say that before you can know anyone, you must peel back the layers and look into their earliest years, because the person we become has already been shaped by the time we're five years old.

Now I don't see the point of talking around it, burying it in euphemisms or avoiding it altogether, so I'll spell it out. When I was four years old my birth mother, Avril, committed suicide. She took herself to the spectacular point where the Pacific Ocean enters Sydney Harbour, and from the craggy, battered beauty of South Head, at the top of a vast cliff known as The Gap, she jumped. She was just 26 years old.

Though I can barely draw a picture of her in my mind, though I can't begin to recapture her smell or the way she might have looked when she laughed, her actions that day, the struggles that led up to that day, and the lingering consequences of that day, shaped me just as surely as the Pacific carved and moulded the very cliff from which she threw herself.

MY DAD, ALEX, WAS BORN AND RAISED IN SCOTLAND, where he worked, predominantly, as a policeman. It was a difficult job then as it is now, and Dad once recounted to me grim days when he had to fish bodies out of lakes or pull people from wrecked cars. And when you were done you'd finish the day not with a police psychologist but with your colleagues, nursing a pint of beer in some smoke-filled pub. That was the extent of debriefing or counselling. The theory was that there was no point talking about how you felt. That was what women did. A man just got on with things. Dad still operates that way and I suppose it's a generational thing.

Dad was once married to a lovely woman called Margaret and together they had three children, Don, Morag and Kenny. When that relationship broke down he wasted little time in marrying my mother, with whom he soon had two children, my older siblings Marc and Marion. In a small town like Rutherglen—which is just outside Glasgow—there was no escaping the gossip this prompted and Dad, I suppose, bore the brunt of it, though clearly it wasn't easy on Margaret or my mother either.

In July 1965, Dad decided to move with Mum, Marc and Marion to the other side of the world: to Australia. Like America, Australia has always been seen as a place of hope and new beginnings, and I'm sure that sounded promising to Dad when he and his young family undertook the long, continent-hopping flight to Sydney.

Ten months later—during which time my family lived in the town of Loftus, which fringes the Royal National Park to Sydney's south—I was born in Sutherland Hospital. Mum was already struggling to cope. The voyage had knocked her around, and she was equally rattled by being separated from her close family. At the same time, Dad was having to work three jobs (as a mail sorter with Esso, a driving instructor and a singer) to generate enough income to keep us happy in our very modest home, which by this stage was in Tregear. This meant, more often than not, that Mum was left alone at home with three children under three.

She began, ever so slowly, to lose her way. First was a period of self-medication when she took uppers to cope with the demands of three squealing, needy children. Then came the downers—and brief periods of hospital care—to balance everything out. Most obviously she was missing not just the practical support but also the emotional connection to her family, and especially her mother. It's a feeling Marc, Marion and I grew to know all too well.

Dad, to his credit, was doing all he knew how to do, which was to provide. But he was an old-school man and I don't think he quite understood what was going on with Mum at the time. I think he was probably resentful that things weren't going to plan. I'm sure Dad was wrestling his own demons, but he'd sooner fly to the moon than talk about them.

At one stage, Mum was unravelling at such a rate it was decided she would go home to Scotland, to visit her family and recuperate. In retrospect, Dad should probably have taken us all back. Australia wasn't good for Mum, that much was clear, though of course it must have been more than just that. I guess I'll never know what was really going on inside her head. But Dad says he couldn't afford to take us all back, and when he asked Mum's parents for financial help, they informed him work was scarce in Scotland and that perhaps the best thing was for her to return to Scotland alone for a short while.

So Mum went alone and Marc, Marion and I were split up and put in different foster homes. Judging by her letters, Mum missed us very much, although the return to Scotland and the reconnection with her family seemed to have lifted her spirits. Yet clearly the situation was unworkable and it was Mum who, after six months, crossed the world again.

Whether it was the journey (Mum returned via ship, a six-week trip from Scotland) or the thought of what was to come we'll never know, but Dad recalls meeting Mum at Circular Quay in Sydney and finding her not the person he remembered. Once she moved back into our simple, fibro home at 9 Penguin Place, she fell apart all over again. She didn't change our nappies, she let the house fall into disarray and she became depressed. She just couldn't cope.

Dad couldn't help but see that something was seriously wrong and at long last Mum began getting more regular help, but it was back to the foster homes for the Maclean kids. Of these, I remember nothing. I did, however, get to meet one of my old foster mothers, Enid Kerr, a few years ago. Enid, who still calls me 'Little Johnny', remembers me as a 'vibrant', if somewhat naughty, kid with a shock of blond hair and an inclination to jump higher and run faster than anyone else. I was craving attention, she said, and I don't suppose there's any wonder why.

Being older, Marc and Marion were occasionally allowed home on weekends, but that stopped altogether as Mum continued to get worse and was eventually admitted to a psychiatric hospital. Diagnosed with schizophrenia, she would, over the next few years, return, time and again, to psychiatric care. Needless to say, Marc, Marion and I had no understanding of what mental illness was, and so it was a very confusing time for us.

Judging by copies of correspondence that my brother secured a few years ago (reports from the foster homes as well as paperwork from various government social workers assigned to us) through the Freedom of Information Act, none of the Macleans was coping too well. Mum, of course, was struggling to deal with her mental illness and her troubled internal dialogue. As adults, we discovered she'd harboured suicidal tendencies for some time and had actually hallucinated about killing us children. This was a very upsetting thing for us to learn and, in our different ways, we've all struggled to take it in.

The correspondence also showed that Dad paid all the foster care bills like clockwork. But he seemed to be disillusioned and struggling emotionally, too. There's a suggestion he was sick of Mum's constant admissions to psychiatric care and had been thinking about leaving her. He also didn't know what to do about his children, and sometimes weeks would go by without him visiting us in care. As for Marc, Marion and I, we were described by our carers as 'disturbed' as often as we were described as 'playful' and 'content'.

On one occasion, Dad was told that Mum had somehow got out of hospital without anyone knowing and that she was found walking around The Gap, a renowned Sydney suicide spot. So Mum was taken back to the hospital and her medical report was amended, making it clear she was never to be released. But I suppose she had already found what she was

BEFORE HE EMIGRATED TO AUSTRALIA, MY FATHER ALEX—HERE, IN 1952, AGED 25—WAS A POLICEMAN
WORKING GLASGOW'S NORTH DIVISION

looking for. The next time Mum managed to escape, she went straight back to The Gap and threw herself to her death.

I can't remember when I discovered the real circumstances behind Mum's death. Marc recalls Dad telling us at the time only that she had died, prematurely, at the psychiatric hospital. Many years later, at age seventeen, Marc discovered the truth from a neighbour, who knew the grim details because he was one of the police divers who retrieved her body.

Marc struggled enormously with the burden of that knowledge and he chose at the time not to inflict it upon Marion and me. I cannot recall when I actually did find out. In any case, the way I rationalise it, Mum wasn't well and, realising she couldn't give us what we needed, she killed herself to give us a new start.

I try to think of it, with twisted logic perhaps, as an act of love.

ABOUT A YEAR LATER Dad married a woman called Anne, the Maclean kids returned home for good, and I turned five. It's about this time that my memories begin. All that happened before this period, if it's in my head at all, is hiding in the furthest corner of the darkest part of my brain. Whether this is due to my accident—either because of head trauma sustained during the accident (which left me unconscious for some time after), or post-traumatic amnesia—I can't say for sure. In any case, I struggle to remember anything before Dad's marriage to Anne, whom I've always called Mum.

From the outside looking in, I'm sure the Macleans seemed a perfectly normal and functional family, and certainly from my point of view at the time I wouldn't have disagreed. How could I know anything different? If you'd asked me then, life was good.

Right from the start I was outgoing and good natured and had boundless energy. I was particularly passionate about sport, which came easily to me. Penguin Place, Tregear, was a small cul-de-sac with just nine homes and it made an ideal space for playing with the neighbourhood kids. Ad-hoc games of cricket, touch football, tennis, you name it, took place on that mushroom-shaped piece of bitumen every weekend and every afternoon after school.

Informal play was a pleasure (if I wasn't finding a neighbour's pool to jump in—whether they were home or not—I was taking myself, quite willingly, out for a jog), but organised sport was even better. I joined school and local rugby league teams, as well as Nepean Little Athletics Club, and I was successful. I was regularly selected in representative football teams and when I was twelve, under the tutelage of coach Kevin Stone, I won a state title in the 1500-metre walk. I was then chosen to represent New South Wales at the national championships at Canberra's Bruce Stadium. Winning that—with Marc looking on and cheering from a grassy hill opposite the stands—was one of the greatest thrills of my young life and I was very proud of myself, even a little cocky. I can recall wearing my New South Wales tracksuit to school after winning the nationals and being lauded in front of the entire school. I felt like the cat that got the cream.

As I learned in my foster homes, jumping higher and running faster than anyone else was the best way, for me at least, to capture some attention. And attention, I must have felt at the time, had to be about the next best thing to love, didn't it?

When I wasn't kicking a ball, I was thinking about it. School for me was about recess, lunch and the long glory of summer holidays when the sun would bake the streets and the days would open up like a ripe piece of fruit, ready to be feasted upon. When I was in class I'd spend my time gazing out the window, either conjuring sporting miracles in my imagination or fantasising about playing rugby league for a living. How good would that be?, I thought. With all this to keep me occupied, my studies, which didn't come anywhere near as easily as sport, fell away. I was no young Einstein. I didn't apply myself to academia and I had my fair share of the cane from the vice-principal.

I'm sure Dad thought of me, at times, as a bit of a smart arse and I'd often find myself out of the good books at home. I remember when I was about eleven, leaving Tregear Public School on my lunch break, running the couple of kilometres home and sneaking into the house to raid a bowl of

JUST TWO YEARS BEFORE SHE KILLED HERSELF, MY BIRTH MOTHER, AVRIL, WAS IN AND
OUT OF PSYCHIATRIC CARE AND SHOWING THE STRAIN. HERE SHE IS IN 1969 WITH ME IN
HER ARMS AND MARC AND MARION BY HER SIDE

50-cent pieces that was kept in Dad and Mum's room. I'd race straight back to school in time to buy myself and my mates some treats from the tuckshop. This was living, I thought.

I should have called it quits after a couple of successful raids, but I couldn't help myself and Dad and Mum soon noticed that the bowl of coins, despite their continued deposits, was getting lighter, not heavier. Silver, of course, is not prone to evaporate so, putting two and two together, Dad confronted me and I made a few feeble attempts to lie my way out of it.

Maybe it was his police experience coming to the fore, but Dad could sniff out a lie from the other side of a piggery and soon his belt was off and making rhythmical contact with my bum. A traditionalist, Dad was never above giving us a flogging and I don't hold this against him at all. He taught us right from wrong; he taught us about respect, about values, and I believe they are lessons that stayed learned. I'm grateful for it.

But that beating wasn't quite enough, and Dad hauled me in to Mt Druitt Police Station where he was working as a building supervisor. He introduced me to a stern, frightening senior sergeant who took me back to the cells and warned me that if I kept up that sort of behaviour this was the kind of place I would see a lot of. I was petrified and never again visited that tempting jar of silver. (By the by, when I told this story to my sister Marion this year, she laughed and told me she also used to help herself to those 50-cent pieces, but I suppose it's too late for Dad to punish her. If there is a statute of limitations on such matters, I regretfully expect it has passed.)

In contrast to me, my brother Marc seemed to have it all. He was academically gifted, he had a string of beautiful girlfriends and he was also a fine athlete, making representative teams and time and again being judged 'best and fairest'. He was everything I wanted to be, and everything Dad and Mum could have hoped for. It was Marc who was going to go on to be a doctor, whereas no-one held such lofty expectations for me. I remember Dad telling me the best I could hope for was a job as a council labourer or a garbage collector.

Needless to say, Marc wasn't as enamoured with me as I was with him. It seems to be the way with big brothers. For example, I recall that while he

ONE OF MY FIRST MEMORIES IS OF ATTENDING DAD'S MARRIAGE TO ANNE AT ROOTY HILL IN 1971. HERE I AM OUTSIDE THE CHURCH WITH A MUCH BETTER DRESSED MARC AND MARION

came to my rescue one day when I was getting beaten up outside the house, he let me take a good deal of punishment before he stepped in and ended the carnage.

On another occasion, which Marc reminded me of recently, we were teenagers and had accompanied Dad to a beach near Botany Bay. He was there to visit an RSL club and finalise details for a singing gig. Dad, I should point out, had spent many years in Scotland as a professional singer, and had even given a show at the famous London Palladium. While he also once sold out his show 'Scotch On The Rocks' at the Sydney Opera House, his singing career never quite took off in Australia in the way I'm sure he dreamed of when he emigrated. Nevertheless, he was kept busy enough on the club circuit and that's what he was busy with that day. Marc and I, meantime, were left to our own devices on the beach.

Showing a less than adoring streak towards me, Marc thought it would be good fun to pick up jellyfish that had been washed onto the sand and throw them at me. He then improved on the idea by actually rubbing them

AGED 10, AT CENTRE, ON MY WAY TO FIRST PLACE IN A 100-METRE SPRINT AT NEPEAN LITTLE ATHLETICS CLUB. I WAS SELDOM HAPPIER THAN WHEN I WAS IN FULL STRIDE

over my torso. I gave as good as I got but it wasn't long before we realised, with horror, that these seemingly harmless gelatinous blobs had stingers— soon we were coming out in welts. In considerable agony, we had to lie on the sand beside each other until the pain subsided.

Many years later, Marc underlined his legend status in my eyes following a misguided boat journey up the Nepean River. Marc, three of his mates and I headed up the river in a runabout to see how far we could go towards Warragamba Dam. An hour later, when we couldn't go any further, we spent the afternoon fooling about on the banks of the river. Finally, when it was time to go home, we discovered, to our dismay, that the boat was out of petrol. Immediately, Marc, who was about sixteen at the time, announced he would go and get help. This meant a gruelling 15-kilometre trip over rocks, through bush, and, occasionally, as he was trying to keep as straight a line as possible, across the river. It took him hours—hours in which we sat shivering and hungry on the sand amid the pitch-black darkness of the bush—before he returned for us, like a conquering hero, on the bow of a police rescue launch.

Marion, on the other hand, was a more mysterious creature to me and we didn't really have a lot to do with each other, particularly in our teenage years. Perhaps it had something to do with stunts like the time a bloke from the navy came around to take her out on a date. Marion was still getting ready, excited at the prospect of a budding romance, and my mate and I started giving the bloke a hard time. 'Are you fair dinkum?' we asked him. 'Do you really want to go out with Marion? Have you any idea what you're letting yourself in for?' And so on. By the time Marion got out of the bathroom, he was gone. We thought that was just about the funniest thing ever. Marion blew her top. I can still see the look on her face.

This is all normal family behaviour, of course, and as I've said, I never thought we were different from any other family. Dad had a job; we had a nice enough house; we played sport, went to school, had lots of mates; there were girlfriends and boyfriends; life was normal.

But underlying this family structure was an unsound foundation. Something had to give.

I FIRST STARTED TO REALISE THINGS WERE FALLING APART when Marc began threatening to leave home. He was just seventeen and would soon be sitting his school leaving certificate. He said to Dad, 'Either she goes,' meaning Mum, 'or I go'. To me, this was like a bomb going off, and our household was never the same again. All the simmering resentments and discontent were brought to the surface.

Being a few years older than me, Marc was the first to articulate the lingering legacy of our birth mother's death. Here was a boy crying out for affection. Dad may have offered us support and given us all the material things we needed, but he couldn't give us the love of a mother. For whatever reason, neither could Anne. Our relationship with her was more pragmatic than emotionally rich. She was a wonderful provider and she did her best to shield us from much of life's unpleasantness, but I never felt she had a strong maternal connection to us, and thus we missed out on everything that connection allows to develop and grow.

For me, the consequences of this have been many. I've touched on some of them already, namely my lack of what's called emotional intelligence and my utter inability to explore, or at least be at ease exploring, my feelings. So when I was lying on my hospital bed facing life as a paraplegic, not only did I not want to look deep inside myself to see what damage had been done, but I also didn't really know how to do it. It's only recently that I've come to recognise this characteristic emotional failing and have attempted to do something about it.

Marc, of course, had his own battles to fight, his own truths to discover, and he did it through religion, joining a born-again Christian church to which he'd been introduced by a friend. Being a perfectionist, he followed its teachings to the letter. He stopped his very promising football career because he wouldn't play on the Sabbath. A one-time heavy-metal fan, he gathered up all his albums, anything with even vague references to the devil, and threw them in the incinerator in our backyard, sending up a pall of acrid, black smoke. To this day he's lived his life according to the tenets of his religion and the Bible. And I admire him for that. That's his strength.

Dad—who has been an atheist since he read in a book at age sixteen that more humans have been slaughtered in the name of religion than in all the wars in history—couldn't cope with Marc's change of lifestyle. While Marc's rejection of football and the football club community bothered Dad, what particularly upset him was the seeming demise of Marc's desire to be a doctor, since, understandably, Marc's studies fell away amid all the turmoil.

I recall us all getting together at a pizza restaurant some time later with friends from the local football club where Marc and I had played. Marion and I had hopes of a reconciliation between Dad and Marc but they were soon dashed. When our food arrived, Marc suggested we pray and give thanks and Dad couldn't take that at all. 'What are you doing with that crap?' Dad asked, and Marc just walked out. It was dark outside and

IN 1973 WITH MARC, DAD, MARION AND ANNE AT THE BOREC HOUSE NIGHTCLUB IN PENRITH, WHERE DAD WAS PERFORMING

positively bucketing down, but Marc headed out into it like you would to a park on a brilliant spring morning. I felt so much love for him in that moment that I left the table and raced outside, running to catch up to him. Silently, as the rain tumbled down, we walked off into the night. I was about fourteen and had no idea what was going on, but I knew nothing Marc had done had changed the way I felt about him.

Eventually a car pulled up beside us, its wipers working frantically. It was Dad, Mum and Marion. Marc and I got in and we all went home together, enduring an agonising silence.

Soon enough, Marc moved out of home for good. Ironically, that saw Marion and I bond for the first time ever as we sought comfort and company in each other. Nevertheless, with Marc having departed in such unhappy circumstances, things were never the same again at 9 Penguin Place.

I FINISHED AT DUNHEVED HIGH SCHOOL in Year 10 and left as the 'junior athlete of the year'. Unfortunately, I also left with an unspectacular academic record. In my School Certificate I scored a four in mathematics and a five—the lowest mark—in English. Clearly, I wasn't going to medical school or into the next space program. All I thought about was getting a car, a simple job and a girlfriend. That was all I really wanted in life.

My first job out of school was at a Safeway supermarket in the suburb of St Marys. Wearing a white shirt, red tie and apron, I spent my days pushing long snakes of supermarket trolleys about the place. I believe 50 was my record. It wasn't exactly my dream and I soon moved into a procession of labouring jobs, mostly on building sites. All the while I was still playing football and excelling, having been selected to play for junior teams representing the Penrith Panthers Rugby League Football Club, whose first-grade side played in the professional New South Wales competition.

I still dreamed of being a first-grade footballer and, as such, a professional athlete. To be paid to play sport seemed to me the ultimate. I'd been delightedly doing it for free all my life so to be offered money to do the same—good money, at that—seemed too good to be true.

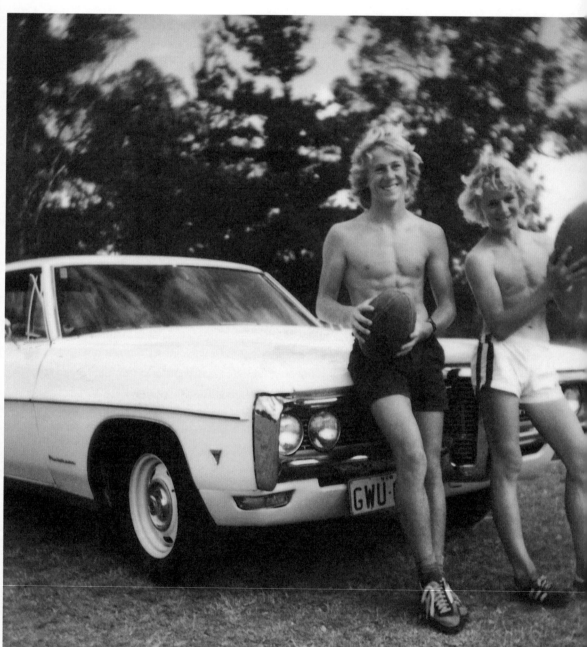

LEANING ON THE BONNET OF DAD'S PONTIAC: MARC, 15, IN PRIME SHAPE, AND ME, 12, HIS EVER-LOYAL SUBJECT

And for a while the plan was looking solid. At 19, I was graded with the Panthers, which means that I was on the club's books and earning a wage. In 1985 and 1986 I played essentially all my football with the under-23s team, stepping up six times to play reserve grade, which was just one step under first grade and the big time. The rise seemed inevitable to me and, with the cocky impetuousness of youth, I warned one of the first-grade wingers that I wanted his spot and, with me being so much faster than him, it would only be a matter of time before I got it.

I learned another lesson in life shortly after that when, in 1986, a new coach took the helm of the under-23s. His name was Graham Murray and he would go on to be a very accomplished first-grade coach, but he and I just seemed to rub each other up the wrong way. Suddenly I was out of favour and, more often than not, left warming the bench. My dream seemed to be slipping away when Graham told me—before the season had even ended—that my services were no longer required.

Initially I was shattered by this, the sudden demolition of my long-held desire. It hurt a little more when my team went on to win the grand final without me. But it didn't take me long to pick myself up. I was still only 20 and I figured I'd just have to lick my wounds in country football and reinvigorate my game, before having another attempt at my first-grade dream. If that didn't work out I was formulating a secondary plan, which was to join the fire brigade, a profession for which I'd always had a lot of respect. And not only because of the rescuing-damsels-in-distress factor.

So I played the 1987 season with Warragamba, travelling some 80 kilometres there and back after my labouring jobs for training twice a week. It was there that I first met Johnno, noting him to be a tough but likeable bloke. Although I arrived with a little swagger in my step (my confidence, long blond hair and fleet feet earned me the nickname 'Hollywood' from the older players), I wasn't an instant hit. Country football took some adjustment. Up against older men as hard and tough as the dry country earth, I got hammered that first year and struggled to find my feet and to recapture the confidence I'd had in my abilities for as long as I could remember.

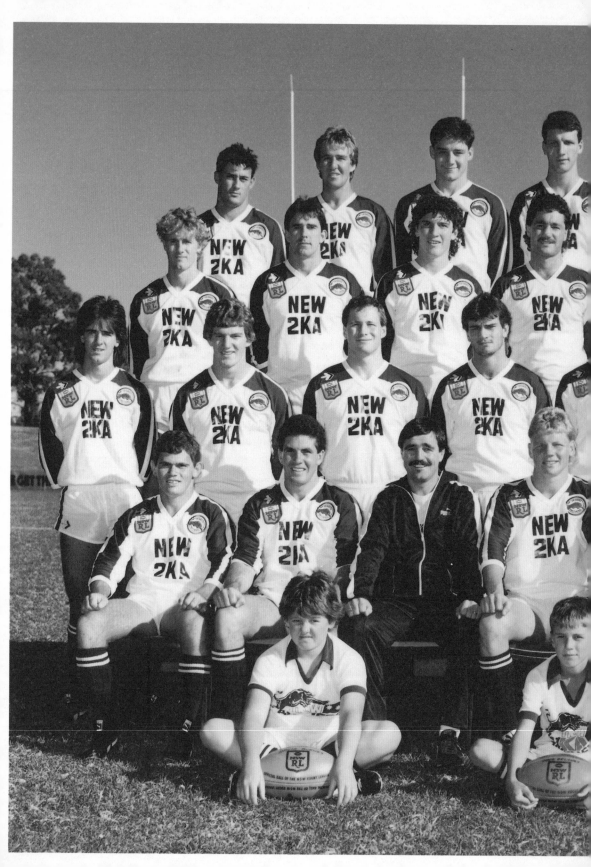

PENRITH DISTRICT RUGBY LEAGUE FOOTBALL CLUB [UNDER-23 GRADE SQUAD, 1986]

THIRD ROW: T CLARKE, R McNEIL, M GEYER, B COLES, J CARTWRIGHT, P AKKARY, J VITANZA

SECOND ROW: J MACLEAN, G MILLER, D LYNCH, D SWANSTON, S WADDELL, G MITCHELL, P SMITH

FIRST ROW: A FITZHENRY, D FERGUSON, C BLAIR, D BURNES, S ANTONELLI, G GIBSON, G NISSEN, J THOMPSON

SEATED: D DELANEY, D JONES, G MURRAY [COACH], C IZZARD, N LOVETT [MANAGER], T PETERS, H SIMMONS

SITTING ON GROUND: G BAILEY, T GAHAGEN, S HANCOCK [ABSENT: J BELL, A BUTTERFIELD]

While I was struggling, I was quickly forming a bond with Johnno, who couldn't believe there was someone who seemed to enjoy training almost as much as he did. I remember one session when Johnno and I arrived early and jumped the fence at the local pool, which was closed for winter. Driving each other on, we swam 40 laps of the 25-metre pool and finished just in time to jump back over the fence and commence training with the rest of the team. Johnno used to say I wasn't too quick in the water, but when it came to running, my feet barely touched the ground.

If season 1987 wasn't much to write home about, 1988 was a cracker. Under coach Mark 'Crocodile' O'Reilly, the brother of the famous Parramatta forward Bill, I thrived, and by mid-season was streets ahead in the team's best and fairest award. The way I was going, I felt confident that a return to the Panthers, or another professional club, was on the horizon.

What with the resurgence of my football dream, a happy relationship with my gorgeous girlfriend, Michelle, and a new full-time job doing maintenance at a local primary school, everything seemed to be going well for me. Add to that the liberating feeling of moving out of home and into Michael's place in Faulconbridge, and life seemed great.

But then a big white truck entered my life and nothing was the same again.

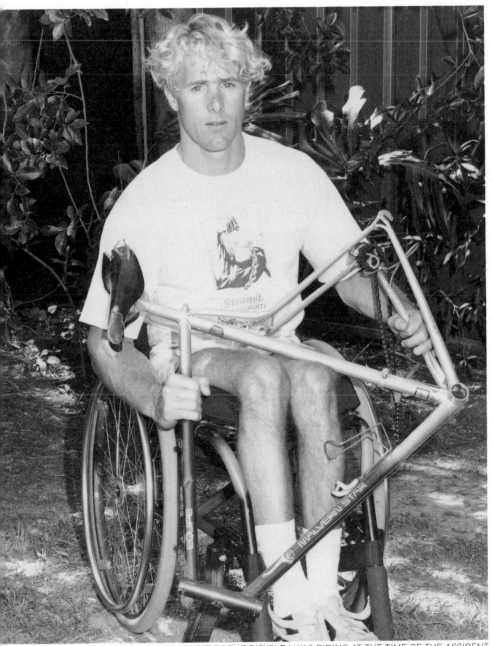

AT HOME IN 1991 WITH THE BUCKLED FRAME OF THE BICYCLE I WAS RIDING AT THE TIME OF THE ACCIDENT

_04

04

TENTATIVE STEPS

WHILE LEAVING HOSPITAL WAS A FORM OF REBIRTH FOR ME, at the time I wasn't so much thinking about a new life and how my second chance could give me the opportunity to reinvent myself. I was thinking about reclaiming everything I had before. I was still only 22 and the future was nebulous. The past I knew. It had clear, definable borders and it seemed good enough. I suppose there's a sense of safety in what you know no matter how imperfect it may be.

It had been arranged that I would begin my post-hospital recuperation living in a rehabilitation centre. Since Moorong Spinal Unit, the formal rehabilitation centre in Ryde, was full (and far from home, in any case), the best option was deemed to be the Governor Phillip Nursing Home in nearby Kingswood. I was obviously still very weak, I was wheelchair-bound, and Dad and Mum's place in Tregear was hardly set up for my special needs. It seemed the best idea.

Within a day I wanted out.

Dad drove me over to Governor Phillip and I felt like a fish out of water from the start. To say the least, the place didn't have the energy I was looking for. To me it seemed dour, bleak and institutional. And, not surprisingly, it was full of old people. I was the youngest there by about 50 years.

There were also many rules to follow and I came up against one within hours. Dad and I had already spoken about him dropping off a dinner consisting primarily of a charcoal chicken, but that idea was knocked on the head when the matron told me it wasn't allowed; I would be eating the nursing home food with the residents. There'd be no special treatment for me.

Shown to my room, I discovered I'd be sharing with two old men. Later that night, as I lay awake in my bed wondering how the hell I had ended up here, one of the men started screaming and got out of bed. He had dementia, the poor bloke, and he was standing there exposing himself in gaping pyjamas and waving a water bottle around his head. It scared the life out of me.

Seeing him in clear distress was disturbing enough, but after he settled down I began to wonder about the rest of my life. I pictured myself as an old man and I wondered if I'd be satisfied that I'd made the most of things, that I'd made a difference and a genuine contribution, rather than just made up the numbers.

In the morning I spoke with Dad and pleaded with him to get me out of there. Seeing the state I was in, he promised he'd make some modifications to the house (principally, install a hand rail to get me up the front steps), pull a few strings and make it happen. Thanks to Dad, that very day I was back at Penguin Place. This wasn't ideal, considering that before the accident I had spent a month appreciating the freedom of being in my own place, but it was infinitely better than the geriatric hospital.

Once at home, Dad began looking after me, and I'll always appreciate what he did for me at this time. When I had my accident I saw part of him soften. For instance, when Dad came to visit me in hospital, he'd massage my feet (Dad knew what he was doing, having helped as a masseur at Penrith Panthers and as a volunteer masseur at many nursing homes). He couldn't just sit. He needed to do something, to express something. To be part of my rehabilitation was a great expression of his love.

As I've mentioned, Dad had experienced a lot of hurt in his life and he tried to deal with it the only way he knew how—by shutting himself off. But my accident, in some ways at least, drew him out of his protective shell. He used to tell me, 'Son, if I could give you my legs I would.' And I know he meant it. It was vital for me to hear and it demonstrated to me Dad's emotional core.

These days, Dad can tell me how much he loves me. Perhaps because of the accident and what I've done since—of which, Dad tells me, he's so very proud—he and I have a slightly different relationship to the one he has with Marc and Marion. That hurts me, because I see how angry and disillusioned Marc and Marion are at everything that has gone before, but I can't change it.

OF THE FIRST THREE YEARS AFTER THE ACCIDENT, I reckon I would have slept for at least two of them. I was out for 16 hours a day. I was constantly exhausted from all the therapy and exercise I was putting myself through in my quest to get everything back, including the use of my legs.

I'd still never been told categorically that I would be a paraplegic for the rest of my life. There was a chance, incredibly slim though it may have been, that my damaged spinal cord would regenerate and allow me the use of my legs again. While, inevitably, I had negative thoughts and sank occasionally into mild depressions, I always maintained a hold on this hope. I constantly told myself that, with the help of Dad and a number of others, including Johnno, I was going to make a complete recovery. Any doubts I may have had I stamped off, like mud caught in the cleats of a pair of football boots.

I suppose you could say I became obsessed, but that's part of my make-up. When I've identified a goal, I go at it with a single-mindedness that shuts everything else out, for better or worse. Little things gave fuel to this determination to walk again. I recall, soon after I returned home, arriving at a local gym in my wheelchair. The gym was owned and run by Ron Oxley, a lovely man who was also a trainer with the Panthers. As I began to regain my upper body strength I started arriving at the gym on crutches. On one of these occasions Ron told me he never wanted to see me back in a wheelchair again. The unspoken but unmistakable message was that this would mean I'd let the accident win, that I'd given in.

With the benefit of hindsight, it was an entirely unreasonable demand, though at the time it gave me the motivation I craved. Like everyone, Ron wanted the best for me and I didn't plan on letting him, or anyone else, down.

While Mum tirelessly cooked and cleaned for me in those early days, Dad devoted himself to me and my recovery. He'd wake me, make me breakfast, drive me to the hydrotherapy pool at Governor Phillip, then to Ron's gym, and, finally, home for lunch. I'd crash out for a few hours before he'd wake me again to do more training, this time in a gym set up in the garage, which had long since become too cluttered for the car. And every evening he would ensure I drank a glass of stout, believing it to have almost medicinal qualities. Dad did all this practically every day for six months.

It was in the early days of this routine that I started to meet—or strengthen my relationship with—all sorts of people who would come to make an indelible mark on my life. These people were mentors to me and without them I wouldn't have achieved half of what I have, or grown in the way I have. Anyone who thinks they can get the most out of life by going it alone is, I think, fooling themselves.

Perhaps it was because I didn't have any other choice, but I learned very early after my accident that it was okay to ask for help and okay to receive it. Being open to help literally changed my life and I could never begin to repay all the people who have made me the man I am today. Not that any of them want to be repaid; their friendship and help were unconditional and I'm humbled by that.

Johnno became a permanent part of my life once I was home. He'd visited me often in hospital and was soon seeing me every day, and I found we fitted together well. He was laconic and grounded, a perfect counterbalance to my often excitable nature.

I'd embarked on a program of weights to build myself up. As well as strengthening my body and reintroducing myself to exercise, which had long been a passion, I recognise now that I was also rebuilding my shattered self-esteem, which had reached a low point the day I saw myself in that hospital mirror. I'd always considered myself a fairly good-looking guy and working on my body helped me to recapture some of my earlier self-confidence.

When I started my gym program, a lot of mates offered to support me, to train with me. I greatly appreciated their offers but they quickly burnt out, such was the unrelenting intensity of my fitness regime (which was tethered to my mantra of 'get it back'). So I was going through training partners left, right and centre when Johnno offered to work out with me. 'I appreciate you coming around and it's a nice offer,' I told him. 'But to be honest I don't think you'll last long.'

This was like waving a red rag at a bull.

Johnno became my training partner and he didn't waver for one second. He wrote training programs with me, he built me weightlifting equipment using his expertise as a fitter and welder, and we set each other challenges, driving each other on and on to the point of exhaustion. For good reason we christened the backyard gym 'the house of pain'.

Naturally enough we were always starving, and Dad and Mum must laugh today to think of us coming inside the house after our marathon weights sessions and tearing the fridge apart. We'd sit at the breakfast bar and devour barbecue chickens, fish fillets and eggs as though we hadn't eaten for a week. And the portions always had to be equal or there'd be no end of complaints. Considering how difficult it is to split a chook perfectly, we spent a lot of this time bickering good-naturedly.

Some time after, to diversify our training, we went halves in a new two-man touring kayak (or TK2) which we christened 'JJ' (as in John and John). With the excitement of kids on Christmas Day, we immediately took JJ down to the Nepean River, got into our swish, newly purchased kayaking clothes, and boarded our vessel at the water's edge. Anyone watching to that point would have thought we were a couple of gun paddlers but, scarcely a second after pushing off and making a few tentative strokes we got the wobbles, causing the kayak to flip over and dump us into the freezing water. While I was untroubled by this after my swimming work at the hydrotherapy pool, it wasn't exactly an auspicious start.

Knowing it was going to take some time to get used to balancing on the kayak—and not wanting each failure to be accompanied by a dunking in the frigid river—I managed to convince a friend at the hydrotherapy pool to allow Johnno and me to take the kayak there to practise. I suppose it was a strange sight for the elderly residents who were down one end of the pool going through their passive movement exercises, but it was great for me and Johnno. At 27 degrees Celsius, the water temperature was a lot more forgiving when, inevitably, we tipped over, time and again.

Eventually, we found our balance and were ready for the river. Typically, there was no subtlety to our first real forays in the water, and we generally flogged ourselves until we could barely lift our arms. The first long paddle we did was up the Nepean Gorge towards Warragamba, the very route Marc, his friends and I had taken the day our boat ran out of petrol. We set off one afternoon, after Johnno had finished work, and we had it in our heads to reach a particular junction in the river before turning back. The kilometres glided by at first, and we barely noticed the sun beginning to drop. But soon the increasing gloom became impossible to ignore. 'Do you think we should turn back?' I asked, worried about the failing light.

'No,' Johnno replied. 'It's just around the corner.'

Not quite. By the time we reached the junction and turned around it was dark. As the minutes ticked by it became increasingly darker, as you'd expect in the middle of a gorge. With visibility so poor, we tried to position the kayak in the middle of the river. It was a strange feeling, dipping our paddles into the black water with our only real sensation of movement being the breeze in our faces.

An hour went by. We began to get cold and, worse, our bums began to ache from sitting for so long on the fibreglass seat. Despite a layer of thick foam, my bum was particularly sore, so we pulled in to shore and scrambled around in the dark to find somewhere to lie down to take the pressure off our tender rears. But when we returned to the kayak, the pain returned within a few minutes and our speed and spirits began to drop.

Johnno's solution to this was to belt out a song at the top of his lungs, and it echoed around the gorge offending every living creature within earshot. It was an inane song about wanting a 'proper cup of coffee from a proper copper coffee pot' and he sang it over and over again. I yelled to him to shut up but he kept it up until, blessedly, we made out a light that we realised was coming from a moored paddle-wheel restaurant. But, heading towards it along the river's edge, we hit a half submerged log and it tipped us into the freezing water. At the same time, whoever was aboard the floating restaurant turned off the light and we were again in total darkness.

Wet, cold and slightly embarrassed, we had no option but to push on, so we nudged the kayak to shore to better enable me to clamber aboard. It was probably another 5 kilometres before we finally saw the lights from the M4, which meant the boat ramp and the car were close. This little episode—actually, it turned out to be a 33-kilometre round trip—typified the gung-ho attitude Johnno and I encouraged in each other at that point in our lives. It also taught us not to paddle too close to a riverbank at night. And I learned, for the first time, how annoying songs about coffee pots can be.

Johnno may have been slightly mad, but he was incredibly giving. We continued with our kayaking on the Nepean River and Johnno always had a significant workload just to get us on the water. Typically, he would store the kayak at his place, which meant he had to get it strapped to the roof of his car on his own. He would then drive over to my house to pick me up. When we reached the river, Johnno would have to unload the kayak and get it in the water, then wait for me to crutch my way down to the water's edge. And when we were done paddling he'd have all this to do again in reverse. He did it day in, day out.

He was the best medicine anyone could have given me at the time, and through the rapport he and I developed, I learned many lessons about respect, about giving and about friendship. And, it being Johnno, most of these lessons I learned through his actions, not through his words. I've said Johnno was a man's man and he's never been one to get all sentimental on me, no matter the situation. I remember one day feeling so overcome with love for him and all he meant to me that I made a bold move.

'You know I love you, don't you mate?'

Johnno just shook his head and gave me a look that told me I'd gone a bit too far.

During this time, at the hydrotherapy pool, I added to my list of training partners when I met Ched Towns, a huge, gregarious father of two, who was working at the pool as an assistant to the physiotherapist. Ched was wearing an Australia tracksuit that day and I discovered he was training for the upcoming 1998 Seoul Paralympics, where he was to compete in the javelin. He was visually impaired. An all-but-blind man throwing a javelin didn't strike me as a brilliant idea but Ched had something about him that suggested he could make a habit of surprising you.

Ched and I started to hang out, first at the hydrotherapy pool, then at the Penrith Lakes, a huge, beautifully landscaped artificial lake built primarily for kayaking and rowing regattas. By this stage I had successfully attained a driver's licence for an adapted car. I still had enough movement in my left foot that it could be used to operate an accelerator and a brake. So I would collect Ched from the pool after his shift and we'd drive down to the Lakes. Ched would carry me to the water, with me acting as his eyes. Tied together by a Velcro leg rope, we'd take off for long swims across the often mirror-smooth surface. I don't know what onlookers must have thought, seeing a visually impaired man carry a paraplegic into a big body of water, but Ched and I were delighted with the arrangement.

Like Johnno, Ched seemed to come into my life at just the right time. This kind of 'coincidence' became a regular occurrence. Every time I felt things had stalled or veered away from the ideal, someone would pop up unannounced to get me back on track or push me into a new and exciting direction. I'm so grateful for this. Why it happened time and again I can't say for sure, but I think it had something to do with the attitude I'd developed, the one about being open to receive help. Thankfully, in my drive to get everything back I didn't go within myself, but opened myself up. I gave people the opportunity to enter my life and many people took up the offer.

ALL THIS TIME I'D CONTINUED TO SEE MICHELLE, and our relationship developed to the point where it just seemed natural to get engaged. I was 23 at the time and I happily went along with it although, to be perfectly honest, I hadn't felt the kind of connection to her I would have liked to feel, or expected to feel, if I was going to get married. At that stage in my life I was clueless about what was needed to make a real, loving relationship work. I'd had plenty of girlfriends, but in terms of my emotional connection to them I didn't do much more than skim along the surface.

Naively, I decided this feeling—or lack of feeling—wasn't that important and I thought, given time, I'd become passionate about Michelle in the way she deserved. So when Michelle suggested we get engaged I agreed, and she went and bought her own engagement ring and I paid her back the money. It wasn't exactly the most romantic moment in history.

In September 1990 we were married at a small church in Lethbridge Park. Colin Thomas was my best man, Johnno and Ched were my groomsmen, and I stood at the top of the aisle, painfully supporting myself with a cane, as Michelle made her entrance. She looked incredibly beautiful and I suppose I must have looked like a stunned mullet.

I don't really know what I was thinking. Here I was, still raw from my accident, not understanding who I was and how I fitted in, and knowing, deep down, that my love for Michelle was grossly inadequate. As it had been with every girlfriend before her. Michelle would one day accuse me of being like a robot, and she was right. Emotionally, that was just what I was.

IT WAS AROUND THIS TIME THAT I WAS FORCED to confront the truth about my condition. It had been more than two years since the accident and, while I'd become bigger and stronger, I hadn't become faster, as Dr Gabrael had assured me I would. I still couldn't walk in any functional way.

I remember being in my bedroom with Dad and pointing this out to him. 'I'm trying as hard as I can, Dad, but it's not happening,' I said, feeling that the dam wall I had my finger stuck in was about to burst open.

WITH JOHNNO'S ASSISTANCE I TAKE UP MY POSITION IN OUR TWO-MAN KAYAK, JJ, ON THE BANKS OF THE NEPEAN RIVER IN 1990

Dad just gave me a look that said he had known all along I would never walk again. Then I got it. The light went on, and I broke down and cried. I was never going to run again. I was never going to walk again. It was the first time since the accident that I admitted to myself the cold truth of the matter. It had always sat there, just below the surface, but I had refused to face it. But as I suddenly saw with total clarity, I'd given it everything, I'd pushed my body as hard as I could, yet my legs had never responded. I was going to be paralysed for the rest of my life.

As I wept, Dad put his arm around my shoulder and spoke to me softly, his words showing me the future was not lost; it just wasn't the one I envisaged. 'But look how far you've come. Now, how far can you go?'

Naturally I was devastated to finally confront the truth about my injuries, but I surprised myself with the speed at which I was able to move on. Dad had left me with a very valid question and it seemed to me to be one worth exploring. 'So, what's next?' I asked myself. 'What does all this mean?'

Up until then, carrying the hope of walking again had been a little like piggy-backing around this old, idealised version of me. But in that one moment with Dad I'd set my old self down and was suddenly lighter. I noted with some regret and sadness the absence of weight, but at the same time felt a new sense of freedom. My quest to get my life back exactly as it was had failed and I had to accept that.

This acceptance played itself out in one very practical way that made an enormous difference to the quality of my life. I used to always struggle around on my crutches, rarely using my wheelchair. Not only was this impractical, in that I could never carry anything and my pace was slow, but given that my legs acted purely as a fulcrum and were not able to take consistent weight, it was also physically exhausting. Surely it was part of the reason I was always so tired.

Until then I'd loathed the wheelchair. It represented everything I was determined not to be. I was going to walk again, after all, so why would I get about in a chair? Coupled with this, I avoided the chair because I didn't want people to look at me and feel sorry for me. I didn't for a second want to give anyone a reason to think I was different, that I was any less of a person than they were. I think the reason I worried they might is that part of me thought so myself. It's why I never wanted to get involved in wheelchair sports in the early days. At the time it seemed an admission that, yes, I wasn't a complete person.

Despite that, the realisation that I wouldn't walk again freed me up to begin using my wheelchair, although I still felt conspicuous and my self-esteem took a battering. Nevertheless, I could make trips carrying things on my lap, and come home fresh instead of wrecked. Because of the chair, my world started to open up a little more.

AMID THE FLURRY OF MY TRAINING came the court case against the insurance company representing the driver of the truck that knocked me down. In an earlier case he'd been found guilty of negligent driving, so it was now a matter of compensation. I remember saying time and again that no money in the world could compensate me for my loss, and that I'd live in a shack and eat potatoes for the rest of my life if it meant getting the use of my legs back. The same holds true today. But that's not how the world works.

As part of the process surrounding the court case, I saw doctors, psychologists and various experts on both sides of the case. Essentially, the insurer was determined to show the court, the Supreme Court of New South Wales, that my injuries—my paraplegia—were not that bad or debilitating. To me they couldn't have seemed much worse.

In the end, the irony was that all my efforts to get back to my old self—the weights, the kayaking, the therapy—acted against me. Physically I looked strong, and the court was told about my active life and how I could get about on crutches. Had I come home from hospital and shut myself off from the world in a depressive funk I dare say I would have received, without question, the maximum amount of compensation at the time.

Some time before the judge brought down his verdict, Dad and I were ushered into a room and my lawyers said an offer (less than the maximum) had been placed on the table by the opposition and they strongly recommended we take it. Dad wanted the case over with and he suggested

THE GORGEOUS MICHELLE STOLE THE SHOW ON OUR WEDDING DAY ON 9 SEPTEMBER 1990

I accept the offer, but I didn't want to. It was not about the money. I felt I was being penalised for doing my best, for making myself as strong as I could possibly be, for using exercise as my therapy and coping mechanism. As a result, I wanted to refuse the offer and see the case through to the end, but Dad was feeling the strain and so we eventually settled.

The driver of the truck never attended court. He'd had his day and been found at fault, but I'd never discovered what was going through his mind that day, how he came to make the mistake he did. Lying in hospital, there were times when I resented him and even hated him for the mistake he'd made, but equally there were times when I tried to see things from his point of view. Whenever I did, I couldn't get around the fact that he never attempted to make contact with me. I'd like to think if our positions had been reversed I would have at least made some effort to say sorry; to say, 'It was an accident, a terrible accident, and I'm so sorry it happened.' But he never did.

After paying my legal team I was left with an amount of money that, to a 22-year-old who thought of himself as essentially a labourer (albeit one who still hoped to play professional rugby league and join the fire brigade), seemed fairly substantial. The money allowed me to buy myself a modified car and an investment townhouse in Penrith, and I can't deny that it made a big difference to my life. But, as I said, I'd give it all back in the blink of an eye just to be able to run again.

I sometimes think of life as a game of cards. When I got hit by that truck I was dealt a hand I would never have chosen for myself, but once those cards were on the table in front of me, I just had to play them out as best I could.

05 BACK IN THE GAME

AFTER RETURNING FROM OUR HONEYMOON, Michelle and I moved into 9 Penguin Place, which we'd bought from my parents. They had shifted to the south coast of New South Wales, to the small coastal village of Culburra, where the pace of life is undemanding and the local bowling club is close at hand. Though my compensation case had yet to be settled, Michelle recalls our first twelve months at Penguin Place as the happiest time of her life.

While I had conceded I wouldn't walk again, I was still driven to be in the best physical condition possible. So each day became indistinguishable from the one before. In the mornings and afternoons I would train with Johnno, Ched and some other mates, while in the early evening I tidied up like a dutiful househusband and prepared dinner, my culinary skills having improved somewhat since I first moved out of home.

If there was any time to spare I would steal a moment on the saxophone, an instrument I fell in love with during my convalescence when Dad, Marion and Michelle surprised me by taking me to see US saxophonist Kenny G at the Sydney Entertainment Centre. Noticing how impressed I was by the music, Dad asked Rex Cottell, the saxophonist in his band, whether he'd tutor me, and Rex was soon giving me weekly lessons on a second-hand sax. I quickly discovered that I wasn't hiding any extraordinary gift for instrumentation, but I learned enough to read music, and I find playing a wonderful form of escapism.

Still, as domestically harmonious as my life appeared, I wasn't entirely satisfied. I had an inkling there was more for me to do; that I had been spared for a reason and I needed to discover what that was. As this still holds true, I believe the feeling was not that I had to complete any specific task, but was more about fulfilling my potential and being the best person I could be. And this, of course, is a life's work. Prior to the accident I never imagined any kind of future beyond playing football, being a fireman, getting married and having kids. While I still wanted all of that, or at least the parts I could have as a paraplegic, I knew there was much more.

During the court case I renewed my acquaintance with Dr John Yeo, then the medical director at Royal North Shore Hospital's spinal unit. Considering how much I'd been helped by him and so many others at the unit, I started to think about giving something back, and I asked him how I might get involved with helping children in wheelchairs.

My timing was perfect. Dr Yeo told me there was an opportunity to join a spinal cord injury awareness and prevention program attached to the hospital. The program employed a few lecturers who had sustained spinal cord injuries and were either paraplegics or quadriplegics. It was their job to visit schools, traffic offender programs and a wide range of community groups to talk about their experiences.

The program soon adopted the name Spinesafe and I became a very happy employee, particularly since I was taken under the wing of senior lecturer Errol Hyde, who had become a paraplegic after a motorcycle accident. A resilient, gentle man—and a mean wheelchair basketballer— Errol taught me the ropes and helped me feel comfortable about relating my experiences with paraplegia to a roomful of strangers. While I've always been relaxed around people I know, there has always been an introvert hiding inside me and I can be particularly anxious when I'm taken out of my social comfort zone. So becoming more comfortable with strangers in such settings was a significant step forward for me.

In my job as a Spinesafe lecturer I would drive around New South Wales talking to people in all spheres of life about the indiscriminate nature of spinal cord injury. Not only did I significantly increase my own knowledge about the intricacies of the spine, but my social confidence flourished too.

Of all my audiences, I most enjoyed speaking to school groups, and I discovered I had an uncanny ability to pick out the inevitable troublemaker before he or she really hit their stride. (Reflecting on my own school history, perhaps it was a case of it takes one to know one.) In any case, I found that inviting the potential troublemaker to the front of the class to help me with a demonstration saved me a lot of grief. Overall, my experiences with Spinesafe were a kind of apprenticeship for the type of speaking engagements I do today.

My time there also reminded me that, relatively speaking, I was lucky in that the nature of my paraplegia allowed me limited movement in my left leg. This was brought home to me by a man I sometimes worked with who was a quadriplegic. Driving him to a job one day, I was astonished to find him becoming antagonistic towards me. He was angry at what I was physically still able to do, and his jealousy and frustration at his own predicament came to the surface.

We can all be envious of people who have something we don't, and in the world of the physically challenged it's as prominent as anywhere else. A quadriplegic may envy a paraplegic. A paraplegic may envy an incomplete paraplegic, and so on. At first I was upset that he could consider me fortunate. 'Would you prefer I broke my neck and was in the same position as you?' I asked him. 'Would that make you happier?' But I began to better understand what was behind his unhappiness and, as difficult as it was to have that conversation, I explained that I was just trying to do the best with what I had. It wasn't what I wanted either: 'Sure I'm better off than you, but I'd prefer to be somewhere else. I'd prefer to be walking.'

SPEAKING TO CHILDREN, INCLUDING DOING SPINAL INJURY AWARENESS EVENTS LIKE THIS ONE, HAS ALWAYS BEEN A PASSION

DURING MY TIME WITH SPINESAFE I didn't reduce my training, I just fitted it in as bookends to my day. At the time, Johnno and I had increased our paddling training and in October 1990 we decided to enter a 111-kilometre kayak race on the Hawkesbury River, a gorgeous stretch of water that wends through Sydney's north. It was my first competitive hit-out since the accident and it wasn't by chance that I'd chosen a kayak event.

Although I was troubled by my backside's hypersensitivity and the lack of stabilising strength in my legs, kayaking was one of the few sports where I could compete at relatively close to the same level as able-bodied athletes. Not confined to a special category, or starting off on a different start line, or with any other concession, Johnno and I, paddling together in a double kayak, were thrown in with everyone else—exactly as I wanted it.

Still very conscious of my condition and a long way from emotionally accepting it, I was determined from the start not to be pigeonholed as a 'disabled athlete', and to this day I am not comfortable with the term. To me it has negative connotations. To 'dis' somebody is to put them down, and that's how the word sounds to me. I am happy with the term 'wheelchair athlete', 'physically challenged athlete' or, simply, 'paraplegic athlete', all of which seem to state things as they are rather than imply, by definition, a less-than-complete person.

Johnno and I were both keyed up for the event, and as Johnno readied the kayak, I used my crutches to negotiate my way to the start line, attracting a few looks which I was keenly attuned to and embarrassed by. But I put it out of my mind as Johnno and I sat in the kayak—me at the front (with very limited rudder control), him at the back—and waited for the starting gun, our support crew of Michelle and Gail looking on. When it did go off, our paddles began churning the water, digging in for purchase, and I felt elated. It wasn't rugby league, but I was back in the game. Back doing what I'd always done best.

They call the race the Hawkesbury Classic, but it's nicknamed Madness by Moonlight and that's an apt description. Starting in the cool of the evening, the race went through the night and, before long, the repetitive motion of paddling, and the effort it took to push the blade through the water over such a distance, had my shoulders burning. The only benefit of that was that my aching shoulders distracted me from my tender bum and throbbing right ankle, which has been locked in place since the accident and is painfully arthritic.

Out of a field of about 100, we finished in twelfth position in 12 hours and 15 minutes. Though a little disappointed at finishing out of the placings, I was charged by my first competitive foray since the accident. And to do it with Johnno by my side—or at least, behind me—was especially gratifying.

NOW THAT I WAS EMPLOYED, my time with Michelle was cut short. As I was away from the house all day, I was fitting in my weights training with Johnno and others after work hours. It became quite a competitive environment and the testosterone, I'm sure, was as thick in the air as fog. As with the kayaking, I could compete as a near equal on all the upper-body exercises and I thrived in this environment, appreciating the camaraderie that continued to rebuild my confidence. Sport was once again becoming my central means of self-expression and definition. It was no coincidence that my favourite workout T-shirt at the time bore the catchcry from Bobby McFerrin's infectious song 'Don't Worry, Be Happy'.

By this time, my compensation money had come through and Michelle and I bought a house near the Nepean River in Penrith. With a pool and a lovely landscaped garden, it was certainly a step up from Penguin Place, and for Michelle in particular, buying the house seemed another solid step in our marriage. We'd been living in the house I grew up in but now we had a place of our own; a place that looked forward rather than one that was rooted in the past.

But the new house didn't change much at all, and I was increasingly neglecting Michelle. Before the Spinesafe job had disrupted my cosy domestic schedule, I'd had dinner waiting on the table for her every night. Now, she was coming home from work and having to cook while I was out back in our new home's large garage, bonding with a bunch of mates over heavy chunks of metal. So focused was I on my training that I didn't see this at all, even when Michelle would get so sick of calling me in for dinner that by the time I made it inside my meal was cold and hers was all but eaten.

It must have hurt Michelle to see that I'd chosen Johnno and sport as the main means of rebuilding my life, rather than her. But, as much as she and I cared for each other, there seemed to be something elemental missing from our relationship. We also had a different view of what the future held for us. Had I got a computer job somewhere (as she'd suggested), and lived a quiet life with a couple of kids, she would have been as happy as could be. Increasingly, however, this wasn't part of my plans. I had a burning desire to do something for myself. I didn't yet know exactly what that was, but I knew it didn't involve me being stuck in an office behind a computer keyboard. Sport, in some way, was to be my salvation. Yet the more I got back into sport the further I moved away from Michelle's domestic dream.

JOHNNO AND I CONTINUED WITH KAYAKING and, after putting in mountains of work, we won the doubles title at the 1992 New South Wales Championships. I'll always remember the faces of some of our competitors when they saw me get out of the kayak and into my wheelchair. Our success at paddling only confirmed in my mind that I was heading in the right direction. But as my rejuvenation progressed, my marriage continued to suffer. Finally, one day in 1994, Michelle said she was going to move out. She'd stuck with me through some of my darkest days and I felt incredibly guilty that I hadn't been able to give her the love she deserved; that I'd been happy and lazy enough to just drift along in the relationship without adding to it. But the more time passed the more I realised that we'd just never had that spark, or at least I'd never felt it.

When Michelle told me she was going to move out, I replied that I wasn't going to hold her back. I said I didn't want her to stay if it meant that, in another few years, she'd realise nothing had changed and then be left to regret that she hadn't got out when she planned. It wasn't the answer she wanted and, before long, my sister Marion, her then husband Tony, and some of Michelle's family were helping her carry her stuff out of our house. Sitting by the pool, I looked on nonchalantly. You'd never have known my marriage was on the brink of collapse. At one point I even asked everyone if they'd like me to get a barbecue going, as if this was a party or something. I was so removed from my emotions that now it embarrasses me to think of it.

As the days, weeks and months went by, I think Michelle expected I'd realise what a fool I'd been and pick up the phone and plead with her to come home, but that was never even close to happening. I was, of course, sad that the relationship had failed but I wasn't in mourning.

Sometimes, when I reflect on my relationship with Michelle, it seems like someone else's life. Here was a loving, attractive person who had given up so much for me and could have been with anyone she wanted. And while part of me yearned for a profound, loving relationship with a partner—something Michelle clearly wanted too—I just didn't feel a connection. If I learned anything about relationships—and I'm certainly no expert—it's that if that connection isn't there from the start it's not going to magically appear.

WHEN I WAS HIT BY THE TRUCK IN 1988 I'd been planning to contest the Nepean Triathlon, a challenging event comprising a 1-kilometre swim, a 40-kilometre cycle and a 12-kilometre run. Early in 1994 I came across a handcycle that had been imported from the USA. A handcycle is generally an elongated three-wheeled bike (the single wheel is at the front) operated by hand pedals at chest level which move in unison, unlike those on a regular bicycle, which are set at 180 degrees to each other.

Seeing the handcycle immediately sparked the possibility of widening my sporting repertoire. As if a light bulb had appeared over my head, I began to think of finishing what I had started: the Nepean Triathlon. I told Johnno the plan; I bought myself the handcycle I'd seen—named the 'Freedom Rider', though it was a 17-kilogram monster—and together we set about shaping our training and energies to meet the demands of the race.

Swimming I'd done enough of, and the 12-kilometre 'run' leg I knew I could handle in my wheelchair on the day, so most of my training was concentrated on building up my strength on the handcycle, a new discipline for me. And so we looked for long, straight stretches of road. Like the M4.

As you might expect, it was with some trepidation that I set out to cycle down a length of the M4, past the exact spot where I'd been struck down. But the first time I did so I felt incredibly satisfied. Part of my life was frozen on that chunk of bitumen, but with every crank of the pedals I was leaving it behind me. 'I'm still here, I didn't die and I'm moving on,' I told myself. It was a defining moment.

Even so, as the race date got closer I began to get cold feet. I felt the significance of entering—it would take me full circle, since I was training for just that event the day I was hit—but, remembering the Hawkesbury River kayak event, I became very self-conscious, anticipating the sideways looks of competitors and imagining their pity.

So one day, I raised a new plan with Johnno: he would help me complete the course (by helping me into the water for the swim, then out of the water and on to my handcycle) but we'd do it the day before the race. That way I could prove to myself that I was capable of completing the challenge without having to subject myself to any undue attention.

MY ROCK, JOHNNO, CARRYING ME OUT OF THE WATER AFTER THE SWIM LEG DURING THE 1994 NEPEAN TRIATHLON

Johnno gave me one of his looks. 'What are you talking about?' he said. 'You're going to do the race with me and everyone else on the day. And that's all there is to it.' He convinced me I had to confront my demons, and I didn't feel I could let him down considering how much he'd already helped me.

On the day of the race I was as nervous as I had ever been. Showing her true spirit, Michelle came down to support me. That meant a lot. But my mind was very much on myself as I waited, with some 1000 competitors, for the race to start. As I feared, there were people looking at me and cameras flashing. I just wanted to get started, to get away from the crowd and into the race and my own head space.

Before the starter's gun fired to send us on our way, Johnno carried me into the water, beside the other competitors, and we wished each other luck. Then the race commenced and we joined the thrashing throng, trying to forge a bit of personal space amid the frenzy. When I got to the end of my swim, there was Johnno. He'd arrived four minutes earlier but had forgone his own best time by waiting for me. Spotting him, I swam onto his back and he struggled with me up the very steep boat ramp and helped me into my handcycle before he went and found his bicycle and rejoined the race.

The rest of the triathlon passed in a bit of a blur and I don't recall too much, except for struggling up a steep hill in my 'day chair' (my everyday wheelchair) during the 'run' leg and being trailed by an ambulance, with the ambulance officers asking me if I was okay or needed help.

By the time I approached the finish line—where I spied Marion and Errol from Spinesafe—a lot of competitors had finished and the crowds had thinned, but I was so happy and proud of myself to have made it. I was certainly still acutely conscious of my physical state, but I was beginning to believe that with my spinal cord injury it wasn't so much a case of what I couldn't do, but what I could do. What I had done was complete a demanding triathlon and it felt good. Actually, it felt fantastic.

Ambition continued to flourish inside me.

IN 1988 WHEN STRUCK DOWN BY THE TRUCK I WAS TRAINING FOR THE NEPEAN TRIATHLON. SIX YEARS LATER I FINALLY GOT TO COMPLETE WHAT I STARTED AND THE RELIEF SHOWS

06 THE ROAD TO HAWAII

HAVING COMPLETED THE HAWKESBURY CLASSIC, the state kayak titles and the Nepean Triathlon, I was now constantly on the lookout for new challenges. I wanted to up the ante.

It helped me, I felt, to set myself a goal to work towards. A goal not only gave my life a comforting structure but I could feel myself becoming gradually more content every time I completed one. As much as I had always loved sport and physically testing myself, I think it was this as much as anything that kept driving me at this time.

With Johnno as support athlete, I entered the Sri Chinmoy, a long and arduous Canberra triathlon comprising a 2.2-kilometre swim, an 80-kilometre cycle and a 20-kilometre run. Instead of my day chair, I borrowed a more streamlined, three-wheeled racing chair and found it made a world of difference. Things didn't go so well in the first 10 kilometres of the cycle leg, however. Then I discovered why—I hadn't fully released the brake, which explained why I wasn't finding the handcycle as zippy as I'd expected.

ENCOURAGED BY A PHOTOGRAPHER, I COMPLETE A SERIES OF PULL-UPS AT HOME
IN LATE 1994 DESPITE BEING STRAPPED IN TO MY WHEELCHAIR

It was an exhausting exercise, but I completed the race without too much difficulty, although Johnno and I discovered we still had much to learn about sports nutrition. We'd set off with nothing more than a bottle of water each, and only through luck found a banana another competitor had dropped on the road. Swooping like a seagull on a hot chip, Johnno picked it up. I briefly argued that since I was the official competitor, the entire banana, and its energy benefits, should be mine alone. But Johnno was having none of that and gave me half, which was better than nothing. I virtually inhaled my share, I was so famished.

As satisfying as it was to finish the Sri Chinmoy, I still had a lingering feeling in my gut that a milestone challenge lay ahead of me. But what would it be?

The answer came soon enough.

Late in 1994 I was at Marion's home watching *Wide World of Sports* on television when one particular segment came on and set off an alarm inside my head. It was a story about the 1994 Hawaiian Ironman, a long-distance triathlon that doubles as the Ironman Triathlon World Championship. The commentary focused on a number of competitors, including American Jon Franks, who was attempting to become the first wheelchair athlete to complete the gruelling race. Just watching Franks battle the course, the elements, and himself, inspired me no end.

Even more motivating, I must admit, was the fact that Franks didn't finish the bicycle leg in the allotted time and was disqualified. He then declined to complete the run leg and finish the race unofficially.

My next challenge couldn't have been made clearer if it had rung my doorbell and slapped me in the face. Here was an opportunity to compete in the 1995 Hawaiian Ironman and become the first wheelchair athlete in the world to finish. That appealed big time to both my competitive nature and my ego.

The more I thought about Hawaii, the more I invested in it. This was arguably the toughest endurance event on the planet and I began to tell myself that if I managed to finish the race I would never again have to question my worth. Not as an athlete and, more significantly, not as a man.

If I actually finished it in the cut-off times required of able-bodied athletes, I felt I could forever inure myself to the pity of others. I would be the equal of anyone walking down the street.

Intellectually, of course, I knew that most people who looked at me were probably just curious and wondering how someone who appeared to be so strong came to be in a wheelchair. I also knew that it shouldn't make a bit of difference what kind of goal I set myself, because any change in my self-esteem had to take place within.

But my gut overruled my brain.

It was a hell of a lot of meaning to invest in a single race (after all, what would it mean if I failed?), but just as I had done when I declared I would walk out of hospital, I felt the need to take myself to the foot of a mountain and challenge myself to climb it. When I think back I can see myself as I was then. Full of pride and determination, sure, but still someone not quite comfortable in his skin; someone who needed to prove something to himself as much as to anyone else.

Coincidentally, because it seemed an obvious progression from triathlon, I had considered taking on an Ironman event before. After completing the Sri Chinmoy I had contacted an official with the Forster Ironman event, on the New South Wales north coast, told him what I had done, and asked if I could enter. Bluntly, he told me no. He said part of the course included a narrow footpath on the vehicular bridge between the twin towns of Forster and Tuncurry and my racing chair would impede runners. I suggested that I could avoid the footpath and be escorted across the bridge on the road by a cyclist or safety car, but he said that would create traffic problems. This was the first time since my accident that I'd been exposed to real discrimination. I was furious. Given my heightened sensitivity, it was an unwelcome reminder that I was considered different.

But then came the epiphany at Marion's house and the Hawaiian Ironman became my sole focus.

Most people would consider *anyone* who wanted to take on this race masochistic at best, and the sanity of competitors has been questioned more than once. An Ironman event, by definition, consists of a 3.8-kilometre swim, a 180-kilometre cycle and a full marathon (42.2 kilometres)—the last of which is usually considered an incredibly testing event in itself. The Hawaiian Ironman is considered the toughest of all Ironman races due to the heat radiating off the lava fields, the spirit-crushing high winds and the long, unremarkable stretches of the course which can test the mind as much as the body.

Devised in 1978 by a group of friends who were arguing over the relative toughness of Oahu's three annual endurance races (respectively involving swimming, cycling and running), the first official Ironman race had fifteen competitors and was won by American taxi driver and fitness fanatic Gordon Haller. Haller won after coming from behind to pass Navy SEAL John Dunbar in the run. Dunbar's crew, after realising they had run out of water, apparently hydrated their athlete with beer, which, you probably don't need to be told, wasn't the brightest move.

In the same race, another bloke from the US armed forces, Commander John Collins (credited with creating the Ironman concept on the back of that argument), completed the race at midnight, having started at 7am. His 17-hour time would later become the cut-off time for athletes to cross the finish line or be disqualified. Apparently, Collins stopped for a bowl of chilli during the bike ride.

Since 1978 the event has become more professional (gone are chilli stops, backpacks and wool bike-seat covers) and it now finds places for about 1500 competitors, which means there are more athletes willing to take on the challenge than there are available places. Because of this, qualifying races around the world are held in the lead-up to the event.

I would discover all this soon enough, but first I set myself the task of completing the Surfers Paradise International Triathlon simply because I'd found out that Franks had raced it the previous year and I wanted to see how my time would compare. With Johnno unavailable due to work and family commitments, I asked David Wells, a mate I'd met through the paddling circuit, to assist me in the Queensland race. Apart from the difficulty in negotiating the short sprint start across the sand to the water (David was allowed to piggy-back me) the race went very well and I was hugely encouraged when I finished in 7 hours; almost 45 minutes ahead of Franks's time the previous year. It gave me the confirmation I needed that I was every bit as capable as Franks of doing Hawaii.

But first I had to qualify. I wrote to Hawaiian Ironman race director Sharron Ackles for details and she replied that to qualify for the 1995 event (in which, as per the previous year, the wheelchair section was a demonstration event) I would have to race off against Franks in the Gulf Coast Triathlon in Panama City, Florida. Whoever finished first in this event—which was held over half-Ironman distances—would get to race Hawaii in October.

I said to David, 'Mate, this is it. Let's do it.'

PANAMA CITY WAS IMPORTANT because it offered me a gateway to Hawaii, but it also turned out to be a place where I would meet numerous people who would play a major part in my life, both practically and emotionally.

One of these was Patrick Connor, an emergency surgery doctor from Chicago, to whom I was introduced during dinner with a reporter a few nights before the Gulf Coast Triathlon. Patrick and I felt an instant rapport and I was soon deep in conversation with him, telling him my story. Even though we clicked, I was still very surprised when, at the end of dinner, he said that if I won the right to race in Hawaii he would assist me financially if I needed it. I had only just met the guy, yet he was offering to sponsor me.

While I was in Florida, my dad was in Canada. As I would soon find out, more doors were about to open. Dad was visiting my brother Don Maclean (no, not the singer of 'American Pie' fame), one of the sons from his first marriage. I had met Don when I was 16, when he and his wife Rita visited Australia, but we hadn't kept in touch.

Obviously Dad had filled him in about me, my accident and my plans to compete in the Hawaiian Ironman, and Don was moved by the account, scarcely able to believe I would contemplate such a race. The first I knew of this was when Don surprised me by calling me in Panama City to tell me he would come and support me in Hawaii if I won admission to the Ironman.

He told me he wanted to help me chase my dream. That was more than enough for me, but Don also reminded me he worked as a union delegate for Canadian Pacific Airlines and said he could help me with flights for race-related reasons. He also said that if I ever wanted to come to Canada and meet my other brother and sister, he would arrange that too.

A few days later, with months and many kilometres of training behind me, I met Jon Franks. Franks, curious to have a new competitor, quizzed me about my swim times. But I'd been around the sporting block a few times and, not wanting to give anything away, simply told him what an honour it was to meet him and how much I admired him after his efforts at the 1994 Hawaiian Ironman.

IN PANAMA CITY, FLORIDA, WITH DAVID WELLS IN 1995. DAVID WAS ALL SET TO SHAVE HIS HEAD, TOO, UNTIL HE SAW HOW I TURNED OUT

Then it was race day. I was feeling strong and confident and I emerged from the water in first place. Not just among the challenged athletes, who had been given a head start to keep us clear of the initial surge during the swim, but of the entire field. So all eyes were on me when David piggy-backed me out of the water and began running across the sand to the transition zone where my handcycle was waiting. Comically, though I wasn't laughing at the time, David stumbled on the uneven surface and, with what felt like the world watching, he and I went crashing face-first into the sand.

With that unplanned slapstick behind me, I dashed off on the cycle leg, still maintaining a slim grip on the race lead. With a police escort and the race leader's car in front of me (complete with oversized digital timer), I felt on top of the world and lapped up the attention. That lasted for another 5 kilometres, at which point the elite athletes on their razor-sharp bicycles shot past me as though I was standing still.

Franks, however—the only man I had to beat over the line—was not among them. In fact, I never saw him on the course after the start and I later discovered, after crossing the finish line, that he pulled out at the conclusion of the bike leg.

This meant that, much to my delight, I had won admission into the 1995 Hawaiian Ironman.

HAWAII WAS NOW ALL I THOUGHT ABOUT, from the moment I woke to the moment I put my head on the pillow at night. In between, training filled my days. Typically, I would wake up and head for the pool (I'd joined a swim squad), then in the afternoon I would go out on my handcycle, incrementally increasing my distances as the Ironman approached.

By this stage, Johnno had married Gail, with me as his proud best man. Yet despite the increasing demands on his time (I'm sure Gail must have been regularly fed up with me), Johnno continued to give me all the support he could; he was as determined to make my Hawaii dream a reality as I was.

For one of our training days, which happened to be Johnno's birthday, the pair of us got permission from the Royal Australian Air Force to use its

Richmond air base in western Sydney to attempt a 180-kilometre bike ride (about 135 kilometres more than I had ever cycled in one go before) without the interruptions of stop lights or the threat of traffic.

We used a tarred 10-kilometre circuit (Johnno stopped to put down a rock after each revolution to remind us of how many laps we'd done), and clocked up the distance in some 8 hours, with Johnno alternating between a normal pushbike and a handcycle just for the hell of it. A *Wide World of Sports* crew filmed a segment on me while we were there, as a preview of my attempt to be the first wheelchair athlete to complete the Ironman. Far from being intimidated by the media presence, I found it actually helped to keep me inspired. I think part of the reason was that the more people who knew about my attempts to complete Hawaii, the more people I would disappoint if I didn't succeed. If I needed extra incentive, that was it.

At the conclusion of our long ride, Johnno and I celebrated his birthday with some jelly snakes. Once again I was in his debt. Imagine giving up your birthday to cycle 180 kilometres.

Johnno was as determined as I was that I'd get over the line in Hawaii, and my sister wasn't far behind. After I'd got through the qualifying race in Panama City, Marion helped me put together a letter which she sent off to Nike. Entitled 'John Maclean: Try Hard' (a play on the word 'triathlon' and a reference to the *Die Hard* movies, in which Bruce Willis plays a character named John McClane), the letter presented a brief biography and requested any form of sponsorship. Much to my surprise, Nike agreed to lend a hand, and sent me bundles of clothing, which I was thrilled about.

A month before the race I flew back to Florida to acclimatise to the conditions I would experience in Hawaii. One of the other friends I had made on my previous trip was Denise Centrone, an attractive young woman who worked for the Gulf Coast Triathlon organising committee. She and I had got on famously and we kept in touch after I returned home. Knowing I was planning to do the Hawaiian Ironman in October, Denise (who lived in nearby Tallahassee but was a regular visitor to Panama City) invited me to stay with her mother, Lynn, and use her Panama City home as a training base. I gratefully took her up on her offer and was quickly made to feel at home by Lynn, a devout Christian who, early on, obviously sensing the chemistry between Denise and me, expressed her wish for me to restrain any urges I might have towards Denise while I was under her roof.

It wasn't easy, but I honoured Lynn's wishes. Denise and I did, however, strike up the beginnings of a relationship before we both decided that living on opposite sides of the world would make things too difficult. That sort of problem has been overcome many times by others, of course, so I suspect part of my reluctance stemmed from my continuing struggle with intimacy. Asking someone to move to the other side of the world to be with me would have been like making a promise I didn't know I could keep.

During my time in Panama City, I planned to get myself a new racing chair, since every one I'd used previously had been a loaner, not one designed specifically for me. I needed something lighter and stronger than I'd had, so I visited a factory called Top End in Florida which, under the guidance of designer Chris Peterson, reputedly built the best racing chairs in the world. They measured me up, made their calculations and, days later, I returned to pick it up.

When they presented me with a bill for $3000 I had no idea what to do with it. Naively—and perhaps arrogantly—I had somehow expected they would sponsor me, although no conversation along those lines ever took place. So there I was waiting to take delivery of my new chair with a bill in my hand, no $3000 in my pocket, and a guy at the desk telling me I wasn't taking the chair anywhere unless I came up with the money.

Then I recalled Dr Patrick Connor and his generous offer, and fished out his card from my wallet. When I got through to him, I sheepishly explained the situation and blushed when he told me to put the man on the phone and not to worry. Patrick gave the guy his credit card details, paid the lot and told me once again not to hesitate if I needed any more help from him. 'I've got to go to surgery now,' he said. 'Good luck for Hawaii.'

Based now in Lynn Centrone's lovely house, I spent my days swimming at the local pool, or out and about on my handcycle or in my new racing chair. During this time I reacquainted myself with Matt Beals, an F15 fighter pilot with the US Air Force. I'd first met Matt in the Gulf Coast Triathlon when he whooshed past me on the cycle leg and shouted out some encouragement: 'Doing great, wheelie. Keep going.'

I yelled out to him that I'd see him on the run. I'm sure he thought that was most unlikely as he increased the distance between us. But, sure enough, I caught him on the run leg and took some pleasure in offering him encouraging words as I smoked by him in my racing chair. 'Keep it up,' I told him, 'and I'll see you at the finish line for a beer.'

Matt and I had that beer, and it was great seeing him again in Panama City. In fact, the longer I stayed, the more social I became. I was thinking less and less about the wheelchair under me, despite the fact, ironically enough, that it probably facilitated many of the connections I was making with people.

My male friends have often wondered why I never seem to have any trouble attracting the opposite sex and I think the wheelchair plays a part. There is something disarming about it, something that makes me unthreatening. I think that, coupled with the gregarious side to my nature which flourishes when I become socially comfortable, allows many women—and people in general—to feel at ease approaching me, or being approached by me.

Certainly something was at play in Panama City. Still, I didn't become friends with just anyone. It wasn't an accident that the people I met had a positive energy about them. For as long as I can remember, but particularly since my accident, I find it difficult to spend time with anyone negative. I'm not a glass-half-empty person and I find negativity exhausting and pointless.

Two weeks out from the Ironman, buoyed by the brilliant time I'd had in Panama City, I flew to Hawaii and was met at the airport by Denise Centrone's brother, Wayne. I stayed with Wayne and his wife, Lee, for a week, and together we went on training sojourns around the Pearl Harbor Naval Station (where Lee worked in the submarine division). The setting was beautiful, particularly when the sun dropped spectacularly to the horizon.

With a week to go, Wayne, Lee and I went to Honolulu airport to meet my incoming team. There was Johnno (Don had organised for Canadian Pacific Airlines to fly him in from Sydney as my coach); Marion; Don; David Wells and his wife, Jodie; David's mum, Anne; a neighbour, Peter Wood; and a paddling friend, Louis McLachlan.

While I was certainly grateful for this amazing show of support, I was too self-absorbed at this stage to appreciate it as fully as I do now. David Wells, his wife, Jodie, and his mother, Anne, for example, had to take out bank loans to be there, while others took holidays from work. It's humbling to think so many were willing to make such sacrifices. I may have taken their efforts for granted at the time, but it did feel like a family had closed in around me and it acted like a fire in my belly.

After a night in Honolulu we all made the short flight to Kona, where the race has taken place since 1980. After checking in, we flew the Australian flag from the hotel balcony and I began counting down the hours until the race, when I would confront my fears and climb my mountain.

Adding to the excitement and nervous energy which each of us felt was my discovery that I'd been chosen by US television network NBC to be one of the athletes featured in its coverage (as Jon Franks had been in 1994). When they started following me around Kona I must admit I felt like an instant celebrity. Rather than make me self-conscious, such positive attention only helped to rejuvenate my recovering self-esteem.

The excitement was building and my destiny, I felt, awaited.

THE PAIN WON'T LAST FOREVER

07

THE PAIN WON'T LAST FOREVER

ON THE MORNING OF THE RACE, I woke before the alarm sounded. It was still dark. I suspect it was the butterflies crashing about in my stomach that stirred me.

Ten months since I'd sat in Marion's loungeroom and watched TV highlights of Jon Franks's gallant but ultimately unsuccessful efforts in 1994, the challenge of the Hawaiian Ironman was finally imminent. Within a couple of hours—just after the sunlight crested the hills and settled on the town of Kona—I would begin a race of 226 kilometres, which would take anywhere between 13 and 17 hours to complete, all going well. It seemed absurd, really, particularly since I couldn't wait to get started.

It made little sense to lie there wondering what the day had in store for me, so I swung into action and slowly, methodically, even meditatively, began dressing. The first step in my preparation was to insert a catheter, something I hadn't dealt with since hospital. If I hadn't fully awoken before, I did now. It's not a pleasant business but I knew it would make the race easier. From the catheter I fed in a thin line of tubing and ran it down my leg and under my racing tights, so as to allow me, in the swim, cycle and run legs, to pass urine without having to stop.

That done, I donned my singlet and black wetsuit, rolling it down to my waist. The wetsuit was the only concession afforded me by the race officials—it would aid my buoyancy, making up, in some small way, for the fact that I couldn't kick my legs like the other competitors.

Before long, family and friends began arriving at my room, creating a wave of expectation that I was happy to ride. Soon we were joined by the NBC news crew and one from Channel Nine Australia, both hoping to get an insight into my state of mind.

'How are you feeling, John?' someone asked me.

'Nervous, mate. But excited,' I replied, not feeling particularly expansive with the race looming.

Finally, it was time to go. Stepping outside was like entering the belly of an enormous substation. I could almost feel the electricity crackling about me from the thousands of athletes and supporters hustling to the start line. Most were half undressed, superbly fit and cut; any fat they may have once had left behind on some road as their training stripped them down to sinew and muscle. I'd first noticed this awesome collection of human specimens in the lead up to the race, as competitors wandered about Kona and put themselves through their paces on sections of the course. It was an atmosphere unlike anything I'd experienced before.

With the race due to start at 7am, I'd given myself enough time to have my race number (00) drawn on my arms, inspect, for the umpteenth time, my handcycle and racing chair, and check the contents of the equipment bags I'd be plundering when my energy reserves inevitably dropped. With everything in order, Johnno and David Wells then escorted me to the narrow end of the funnel-shaped harbour where the race would begin. Picking me up, one on either side, they carried me across the sand where all the athletes were gathering. Through the throng, we made our way to the gently slapping ocean and Johnno and David waded out until it was deep enough to drop me into the warm, calm water. To have Johnno and

THE CALM BEFORE THE STORM: WAITING FOR THE START OF THE 1995 HAWAIIAN IRONMAN, SUPPORTED
BY DAVID WELLS (LEFT) AND JOHNNO (RIGHT), BOTH IN WHITE BASEBALL CAPS

David be a part of this, considering all they'd done to help get me here, was incredibly special and I think we could all feel that. But typically, few words passed between us.

In any case, the time for talking was over.

Then someone yelled at me accusingly, 'Hey, why are you in a wetsuit?'.

Gordon Bell, a fellow competitor (and a bloke I knew well from the Nepean Triathlon Club at home), answered for me. 'He's in a wheelchair, you idiot.'

That shut the heckler up.

By this stage 1500-odd athletes were crowding about, shuffling, stamping and snorting in the water, ready to go. Along the foreshore and jetty stood thousands of expectant spectators, lit by the morning sun, which had begun burning off the thin blanket of mist that lay over the foothills outside town. Helicopters buzzed overhead and I knew a small cannon was being readied on the pier; when it discharged, all the pent-up energy in the water was going to be released in an explosion.

And that's what happened.

BEFORE THE SMALL CLOUD OF SMOKE FROM THE CANNON could disappear, the sea was a mass of whitewater, churned by flailing arms and legs, as competitors quite literally swam over each other. It's not uncommon for people to get broken noses at the start of a triathlon swim leg and I was conscious of keeping out of trouble, setting myself a wider, less direct route that would protect me from the masses.

I was sensible enough for that but it was difficult, what with the expectation and adrenaline surging through me, to go out anything but hard—before I even reached the turnaround marker (a spectator boat) I was gasping for air. This is ridiculous, I said to myself, you've only started.

But once around the marker I found a rhythm and a little more space and headed back for shore, following a line of bright orange marker buoys anchored to the sea bed. I was unable to think of much more than keeping my stroke together, keeping it fluid. Every now and then, small fish would dart under me in the clear water and their presence was a welcome, if brief, distraction.

With 1.9 kilometres completed, the thrashing ball had begun unravelling into a series of lines as the stronger swimmers began to pull away from the field. I felt I was in a good strong position, and little waves began to form around me, giving me a small lift and carrying me towards the shore, which was marked by the columns of palm trees sticking out above the roofs of the town.

I completed the swim leg in 1 hour and 7 minutes, well within the 2-hour 20-minute cut-off time. With the elite taking some 50 minutes, I was very happy with my time and felt supremely confident that, apart from the expected discomfort, I would have no trouble completing the course by midnight. I had roughly 9 hours and 20 minutes in which to complete the 180-kilometre cycle leg if I was to continue in the race.

I was one of only a handful of athletes not wearing an orange cap (my blue cap allowed NBC to more easily follow my progress through the race), so Johnno and David—my legs—could see me coming and were waiting waist-deep in the water to lift me out and carry me up a boat ramp, the swim's exit point.

Once in the transition zone—a hive of activity as athletes rushed about to get out of their swimwear and onto their bikes with as little time wasted as possible—Johnno and David helped peel me out of my wetsuit, carried me through a shower to wash off the salt water, and helped me get ready for the long bike leg. I donned my helmet, sunglasses and shoes while I was slathered with sunscreen and had Vaseline smeared under my arms to prevent chafing. For good measure, David also rubbed Vaseline across the back of my neck. None of us considered at the time how badly matched were Vaseline, skin and intense Hawaiian sunlight.

On any other day I would follow up a 3.8-kilometre swim with a large breakfast and a sleepy sense of satisfaction. This time I was getting on my bike—with my legs stretched out in front of me—preparing for so much more. But despite the long swim, I was feeling pretty strong as Johnno slapped me on the back and I began cycling out of the transition zone and onto the road, which was lined with screaming spectators, all of whom seemed to give their lungs a good clear out when they saw me coming.

Their encouragement filled my sails and helped me overcome the long, demanding hill that would take me out of Kona. As I had discovered, every rise in the road seems considerably tougher when you're on a handcycle than it does on a bicycle. By using arms rather than legs, a wheelchair athlete is using a smaller muscle group, which just can't take the kind of punishment a big pair of thighs can handle. Couple that with the fact I'd just swum 3.8 kilometres and I got my first hint that perhaps this cycle leg wasn't going to be as comfortable as I'd expected.

But I was soon over the top and saw the Queen Kaahumanu Highway (the Queen K, for short) unfurled like a hall runner to the horizon, its end point shimmering in the heat. Another surge of adrenaline raced through my veins. I felt elated. Here I was in the world's toughest race. I'd lined up on the start line with everyone else. I was undertaking the same course as everyone else and I would finish on the same line as everyone else, getting through under the able-bodied cut-off times if everything went according to plan. Try telling me after that that I was any less of a person, despite the loss of my legs.

The buzz I was feeling continued as cyclists zipped past me, people shouted encouragement ('C'mon wheelie!') and the Channel Nine camera crew pulled up beside me for an on-the-go interview. 'How you doing, John?'

'What a beautiful day,' I replied, the picture of comfort, before adding, 'Hi, Mum!'

Then everything changed. Just like that.

ONE REASON THE HAWAIIAN IRONMAN is considered one of the toughest endurance events in the world is the heat. When you're out on the Queen K, which is lined with black volcanic rubble and precious little else, you don't just feel the heat belting down on you, you also feel it coming up at you in waves. With my handcycle so low to the ground I felt it keenly. But the heat is nothing compared to the wind.

MY BROTHER DON COULD AFFORD TO SMILE, BUT I WAS DOING IT MUCH HARDER OUT ON THE QUEEN KAAHUMANU HIGHWAY DURING THE CYCLE LEG OF THE 1995 HAWAIIAN IRONMAN

When I began the cycle leg, the conditions seemed kind. I'd heard many times that in October the trade winds could hit you on the Queen K and make life very unpleasant. But the gods seemed to be smiling and what wind I did notice was as gentle as the lick of a cat.

About an hour into the cycle leg a gust hit me head on and my speed nearly halved. What was already difficult became doubly so. Later I would hear that at times the wind topped 100 kilometres per hour—the worst in more than ten years of the race—and was blowing competitors off their bikes. But I didn't need a speed reading to judge its strength. I noted with despair that I had to pedal in my easiest gear—the gear I'd normally use to go up the steepest hill—to get down the next decline I came to.

In a heartbeat I'd gone from 'Hi, Mum' to 'Welcome to Ironman'.

Suddenly the stretch of road before me was ominously long and forbidding. Apart from a few rolling hills, it was monotonous. I'd fix on a point in the distance and it would seem to take forever to get there. And all the while the heat intensified and the wind howled. Proficient cyclists were by now zooming past me, accentuating the difficulty I was experiencing. For the first time I began to worry about making that cut-off time.

Feeling my energy and resolve inexorably draining, I tried to stay positive, to recapture the feelings I'd had seemingly moments ago. But with every revolution of my arms, with every bicycle that passed me, I was diminished. It felt as though my competitors and the elements were pecking away at me, slowly but steadily reducing me to an empty shell.

Thankfully, there was a respite every 10 kilometres, when I'd reach an aid station. There, competitors were offered water, energy drinks, carbohydrate gels, lollies and bananas, anything to replenish dropping energy stores. Almost as beneficial were the aid-station volunteers themselves, who handed out cheers and encouragement with the food and drink. I can't begin to tell you what a difference this made. But once I'd left the aid station behind in a mess of dropped sponges and water bottles, the road and the landscape enveloped me again in their hot, windy, vast nothingness.

By this stage the wind seemed to have picked up even more, if that was possible, and even downhill sections offered no relief. My shoulders began to ache. Making things worse, the elite athletes—the likes of German Thomas Hellriegel and Ironman legends American Mark Allen and Greg Welch from Australia—had rounded the halfway point in the Queen K and were on their way back on the other side of the road. Heralded by helicopters and Harley-Davidsons, they were pushed by the wind and seemed, at least in comparison to me, to be flying.

Loneliness began to prey on me and my triceps began to cramp. A few times I allowed my thoughts to focus on my legs, all skinny and useless and stretched out before me. How much easier would this be if I still had them, I wondered, before asking myself if I'd even be here if I hadn't had the accident. But it was difficult to let my mind wander because of the spasms now assailing my arms. I thought about pulling over and giving them a rest, massaging them myself, but I worried that if I did they'd lock up and I'd never get them going again.

So I pushed on into the wind. Into the heat. This race was beginning to seem barbaric.

It took me five hours to reach the quaint town of Hawi, the halfway stage and turnaround point in the cycle leg. My timing could have been better.

As many other athletes with and behind me discovered, the cruellest thing about the trade winds is that in the early afternoon they turn on themselves 180 degrees. Thus, soon after rounding the halfway point and heading back to Kona, the wind shifted and was again blowing in my face.

That all but destroyed me, yet somehow, aching and hollow, my arms kept cranking. Around and around. And slowly, all too slowly, the road crept by beneath me, the mile markers taking an age to appear. And when they did appear it was only to taunt me, reminding me just how far I still had to go.

By mid-afternoon I could see the sun was well into its downward arc and I knew I was in real danger of not making the transition cut-off by 5.30pm. I'd momentarily seen Johnno, David and Don out on the course, waving Australian flags, and I knew I was in trouble when the sight failed to give me a burst of positive energy.

Essentially, I was in a world of pain. I'd had no real idea what this course could throw at me and now I was finding out in no uncertain terms. Of course, it was nothing even remotely like the pain I experienced after my accident, but nevertheless I recognised it as one of those times in my life when I felt stripped down. When my mask was torn off, and the fronts I used to get through every day were ripped away. And what I was left with was the bare essence of myself. They say you find yourself on the Queen K. Truer words have never been spoken.

When that happened to me in the hospital, when I wheeled past that mirror and saw my devastated body for the first time, I interpreted this bare essence as something distasteful and ugly, such was my shock. This time, it felt as though I stripped everything away only to find nothing inside, a big empty hole.

But there was something, somewhere, for my arms kept cranking.

When the road ran down to overlook the ocean and I saw the way the light angled across it, I again contemplated the looming cut-off time and, from somewhere within, rallied for one last go. I just had to make it so I could undertake the run leg and finish the race legitimately.

I couldn't stop the sun falling, however, and when I was still cycling in the creeping twilight I knew I'd run out of time. Coming into Kona, I again caught sight of Johnno, and I can only imagine I gave him a look of utter despair. I had simply run out of energy. My arms were cramping and in total discomfort, my underarms were chafing, the extreme sunburn on my neck and shoulders was stinging and I was staring failure in the face.

Like Jon Franks the previous year, I was not going to get through the bike leg in time. And, like Franks, I knew that when the race president, David Yates, met me at the transition and asked me to continue anyway, just so they could see in what sort of time a wheelchair athlete could reasonably be expected to finish the event, I would decline. I was gone on all fronts. There was no way in heaven or hell that I was going to reach that transition and undertake my first-ever marathon, another 42.2 kilometres on the road. All I wanted was to get home, dig a big hole and climb in.

With about 1 kilometre to go in the cycle leg, I reached the last hill before making the transition zone. By the side of the road stood Johnno, who'd run across a golf course to meet me. Initially, he said nothing and I cranked painfully slowly up the hill. Finally he spoke. 'Mate, you've been disqualified. But they're going to let you go on. To finish.'

'Johnno, I'm gone,' I told him. 'I'm completely gone. I've got nothing left. I'm not going on.'

And still he walked slowly beside me as I struggled up the hill, silent again.

Johnno meant so much to me after all we'd been through together: football, my time in hospital, recuperation, weight training, paddling. He'd been with me every step, pushing me to reclaim my life when I could easily have slipped into depression and self-loathing.

Now I just wanted him to go away. I was feeling terribly sorry for myself and I wanted to wallow in it alone.

Then he broke the silence and, just as when that first burst of wind hit me in the face with the strength of a gloved fist, everything changed again.

'John, you've got to go on,' he said, not pleading, but ordering. 'It's my son's birthday today but I came here to support you. You've got to go on.'

It was close to dark now but I could see tears in his eyes; I could see he was feeling for me and hurting because he couldn't physically help me (if he did, I'd be disqualified). But with those few words he expressed how much this meant to him, and that affected me deeply. Effectively, he was saying, 'How dare you stop? How can you give up on me?'

With those few words Johnno reached over, ripped my chest apart, grabbed hold of my heart, squeezed it, and told me, 'You're going to have to give a bit more.'

FROM THINKING THERE WAS NO WAY I COULD GO ON, I was now thinking there was no way I could not. I didn't reply to Johnno but my heart had decided that I'd do anything for him because of what he'd done for me.

So I pushed on silently up and over the hill and rolled blissfully down the other side. Finally, after more than 10 hours on my handcycle, I reached the transition zone. There, as expected, race president David Yates confirmed my worst fears.

'I'm sorry, John, we have to disqualify you. You're 40 minutes too late. But we'd like you to continue anyway, to see whether this course can be completed by a wheelchair athlete.'

Thinking of Johnno I replied, 'Okay, I'm going on.'

By this time Johnno had caught up with me and, with David's help, lifted me into my racing chair. For a moment I sat there doing nothing. The cameras were on me, everyone was looking at me, and all I could do was sit and try to compose myself. I was about to start my first-ever marathon, despite feeling I would struggle to wheel the length of a basketball court.

And then, painfully slowly, I was off again.

It was totally dark now and I had small green glow sticks hanging from my chair. Other athletes coming through the transition had them pinned to their clothing, creating a surreal sight as they ran off and into the night, the luminous rods swinging around violently as if suspended in mid-air.

Initially, I didn't need glow rods to be seen. The NBC cameras were still on me, documenting my pain, and I was led off by two Harley-Davidsons. I soon wished I was aboard one because almost immediately I hit a long, steep hill. At that moment it seemed like a cliff face.

I found the going all but impossible. The length and design of the racing chair meant that as the hill's gradient increased, the front wheel would lift off the ground every time I tried to push forward. At times I thought it would shoot right up and topple me out. And if that happened I was not getting back in. I tried to persevere but I was getting nowhere and there was nothing left in my arms, which had taken me all this way. It was as if they were made out of licorice.

In a panic I turned to Johnno and David, who had decided to walk along beside me for the hilly first kilometre of the run leg. 'I can't go any further,' I said. It was an apology.

David made a suggestion. 'Turn the chair around and go up backwards.'

With nothing to lose, I turned the chair to the side, removed my gloves, redirected the chair so it faced downhill and, using the small push rim on the outside of the wheels, I inched my way backwards up the hill, eventually, after an age, reaching the top.

Ahead of me was a long downhill run and—was this someone's idea of a joke? I thought—another hill.

I got partly up it tail-first, but then had to stop. I just knew my race was over. I could go no further. I was wrecked, ruined and empty. Johnno had met me at the foot of this second hill and had been walking along beside me at the time. 'I'm not enjoying this anymore,' I said, stating the obvious, trying to convince him to let me stop. He only needed to say the word.

But he didn't. Again he found something inside me I didn't know was there. With a wry smile he said: 'The pain won't last forever, but the memories will.'

It's incredible to me to think how our brains—or is it our hearts?—are linked to our bodies. For the second time in half an hour I had made a genuine assessment of my physical state and both times I had come away utterly convinced I was depleted of all energy. My tank was empty. You can fiddle around with a car's circuitry and engine all you like but if there's no petrol in the tank there's no petrol in the tank. It constantly amazes me, but the human body is different.

So again Johnno lit a fire within me: the pain won't last forever, but the memories will.

I couldn't help but smile when he said it. 'Get that on tape, brothers,' I said to a film crew, 'that was beautiful.'

Suddenly my spirits were lifted, my arms felt rejuvenated and I had the strength to go on. How did this happen? How did Johnno twice find some reserve of resolve in me, a resolve that could override the fact I was physically spent? I had no idea but on I went. And, incredibly, the more distance I began to cover the more convinced I became that I would make it.

I swept through the downhills, almost euphoric at the wind-whistling ease of it, and found enough strength to battle up the other side. For the first time in ages I seemed to be gaining ground rather than going backwards. I was passing runners—who had wished me luck as they zipped past me on the bike leg—and picking up places, and, in the dying wind, rolling along with a relative ease that seemed to contradict everything that had happened before.

As I reached the turnaround point of the marathon, I felt for the first time that I was homeward bound and my heart lifted at the thought. Compared to the handcycle leg, I fairly rocketed along, leading home the pair of Harleys which lit up the road ahead of me while their riders blew whistles to alert spectators that I was coming through.

A few hours later, hours in which my brain shut down and my will took over, I could again see the lights of Kona and I knew I was getting close. Then the number of spectators along the road started to increase.

Seeing them, I was reminded of the camaraderie that exists within the triathlon community. There's a certain spirit among its members. While it appreciates winners, like every other sport, it equally appreciates competitors. So not only were these spectators family and friends of athletes yet to finish the race, they were also athletes who'd already finished the race themselves and, despite their obvious fatigue, had stayed to clap on those behind them. They could have been lying in a deep hot bath in their hotels, but instead they were behind the barricades cheering and encouraging with everyone else.

The closer I got to the finish, the thicker the crowds and the louder their roars became, and the more I could feel my exhaustion drop off the back of my wheelchair like ballast. With about 600 metres to go, I applied my brakes for the first time. Why would I rush this and get it over with? Slowing down even more, I removed my gloves just as two girls ran onto the course and asked me if they could give me a hug. What do you say when two buxom Californian blondes ask if they can hug you but, 'Absolutely. Go for your life.'

Alii Drive and the finishing chute now lay before me and I all but dawdled to the line as I removed a small Australian flag from my racing chair and waved it proudly in my hand. David Wells's wife, Jodie, then leaned over the barricade and gave me a kiss. Everyone was looking at me and cheering. I could feel their support, well wishes and affection surging into me and I wanted to soak it up. I knew I was never coming back so I wanted to make the most of it.

I suppose my overwhelming feeling was one of pride. I was proud to be Australian, and proud that I'd climbed this mountain. I'd finished the race in

14 hours and 52 minutes—2 hours and 8 minutes before the midnight deadline—and I'd done so despite twice being utterly convinced I was finished. My mind wandered ever so briefly back to hospital and I could only smile, as the cheering continued, at the contrast between then and now.

With my adrenaline pumping and music blaring and people shouting and screaming, I pulled up at the finish line, feeling on top of the world, knowing it couldn't get any better than this. To end my race and emulate Australian Greg Welch, who jumped in the air when he won the 1994 Ironman, I popped a wheelie. Ever the showman.

Ahead of me was an IV drip, a massage and a reacquaintance with pain, but in the moment I crossed the line that was out of my mind entirely. Marion was there to give me a hug, and while I wasn't eligible to receive an official finisher's medal, Don slipped a flower lei around my neck instead.

And there was Johnno. As always, there was Johnno. And he leaned towards me and gave me a pat on the back. No emotion, no hug, just a pat on the back—and a few brief words.

'You done good.'

AN OFFICIAL PHOTOGRAPH SHOWING ME CROSSING THE FINISH LINE AT THE 1995 HAWAIIAN IRONMAN

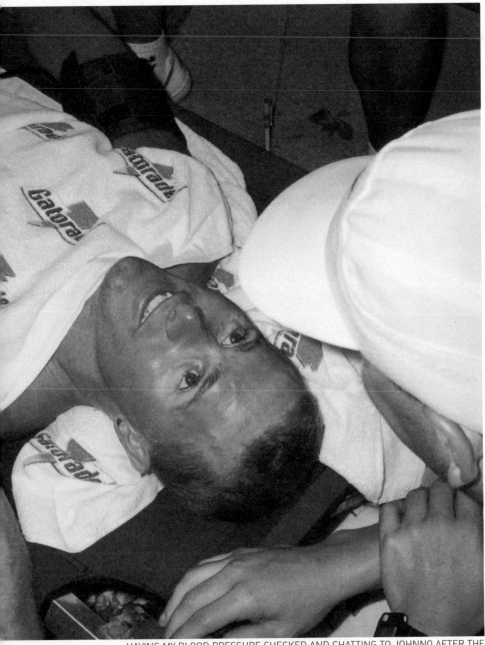

HAVING MY BLOOD PRESSURE CHECKED AND CHATTING TO JOHNNO AFTER THE
1995 IRONMAN. THE EXPRESSION ON MY FACE TELLS THE STORY

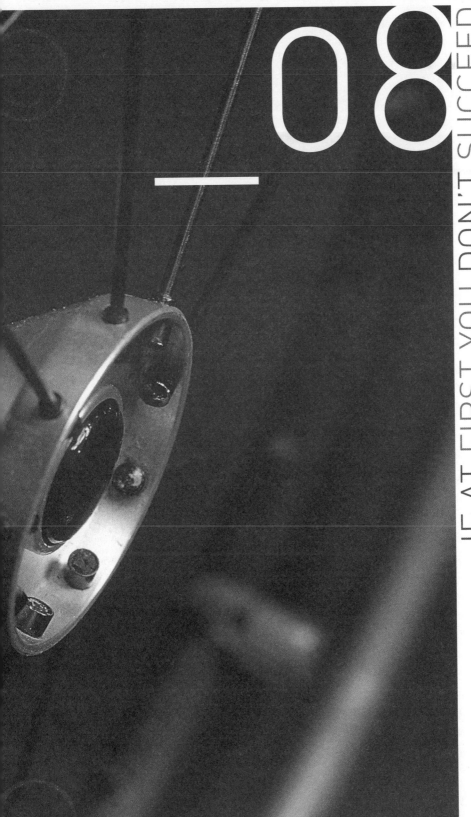

IF AT FIRST YOU DON'T SUCCEED

08 IF AT FIRST YOU DON'T SUCCEED

THE FOLLOWING MORNING I WOKE FEELING INCAPABLE of movement. Even blinking seemed exhausting, and I couldn't have buttered a slice of bread, so wasted were my arms and shoulders. Out and about in my chair later that day, I asked Johnno to hold my hand and tow me like a busted car, but this raised his eyebrows and challenged his masculinity. So, instead of his hand, I held on to the back pocket of his jeans and let him pull me around Kona so I could bask in the beautiful afterglow of the race.

Many people recognised me on the streets and were quick to pass on their congratulations and admiration, which was lovely. One fellow competitor, Theresa Small, made me an offer which was all the more extraordinary considering I'd never met her before. 'Out on the lava fields of the Queen K I was really hurting, but when I saw you, John, I didn't feel so bad anymore. You really put my own pain into perspective and motivated me to keep going. So thanks. But I heard you didn't get your [finisher's] medal and I want to give you mine,' she said.

It was an incredibly touching gesture but obviously not one I could accept. 'Thank you so much, but you raced and you deserve it. It's your medal,' I told her.

Then we bumped into Steve Petite, a bloke I met briefly during the Gulf Coast Triathlon in Panama City. He made another generous offer. 'John, I've been looking for you everywhere. I've got some great news. I'm getting married today and, guess what? You're the best man. What do you say?'

I barely knew the guy, but what could I say except okay? So, at sunset, my entire team came along with me to the beach where the wedding was to be held. Johnno and David carried me across the sand so I could receive the ring from Steve for safekeeping and take my place until I was called into action. Margie, Steve's bride to be, was radiant in a dress she'd picked up at a charity shop, while Steve wore a white shirt and a pair of shorts. When the time came, I did my bit and handed Steve the ring as the sun was extinguished spectacularly in the Pacific. It was a very special occasion, if slightly bizarre considering how it all came about.

That night there was, as is the custom, an Ironman presentation evening. And while I didn't officially finish the race I was, much to my surprise, called up on stage simply to let the crowd acknowledge me, which they did with a spirit I'll never forget. I thanked them for all their support, and told them to keep reaching for their goals.

It was a perfect, if somewhat unexpected, way to say goodbye to Hawaii.

A FEW DAYS LATER, I RETURNED TO SYDNEY and my empty house. After the excitement of the previous month it was certainly anticlimactic. The race had taken so much out of me physically and emotionally that I spent the best part of six weeks recovering, some days doing little more than sleep, eat and reflect on what I had done and what it meant.

In the early stages I had no doubts that, despite being technically disqualified, I had, by finishing the race, achieved everything I'd set out to do. Yes, I had told myself that I could only be truly satisfied, and that I would only be considered 'equal', if I completed the race within the cut-off times.

But after going through what I did to get to the finish line, it seemed ridiculous to hold myself to such a technicality. I'd persevered through considerable pain and I'd come out the other end. I had no doubt then—and I have no doubt now—finishing that Ironman was my life's greatest triumph.

What increased my pleasure was recognising the benefits (benefits broader than my return to health) that had come from my journey to Hawaii. Since hobbling out of the hospital I had continued to build around me a group of people—family and friends—who supported me. They were like the retaining walls in my life; without them I might have caved in on myself.

On a more practical level, I had also begun to attract the interest of financial supporters and sponsors. Their generosity meant that perhaps I could become a professional athlete, as I'd always dreamed. Certainly it would be ironic, considering I was now a paraplegic, but that brought its own satisfaction.

Most importantly, completing Hawaii allowed me to feel more comfortable in my body. I say 'more comfortable' because I imagine this to be an ongoing journey. Part of the reason for taking on the Ironman was to prove to myself that I was whole: that, despite the loss of my leg function, I was as complete a person as anyone else. And after coming home that's certainly how I felt.

Through talking to many Ironman 'graduates' I've found that the race often serves that purpose. Many people questioning themselves and their worth have been altered by overcoming the significant physical and mental challenges of an event like Hawaii. Getting through Ironman has given them the strength and confidence to face other challenges in their life. They've created an important, life-affirming precedent that they can draw on when the going gets tough.

Of course, taking on an Ironman is not something everyone wants to do. But what I've found is that taking on and overcoming challenges in any form—be it the challenge to learn a musical instrument, or write a book, or be a better uncle—makes us all better people. I happened to use sport as my main outlet, because that's what I knew and loved, but for another person it may be something else entirely.

In any case, completing Hawaii changed something in me. Less and less did I think of myself in terms of my condition. Nor was I as quick to reduce my definition of myself to my physical state. If there was one demonstrable example of my shift in attitude that followed Hawaii 1995, it was pursuing a serious interest in wheelchair basketball. To think that I'd once eschewed any kind of wheelchair use outside of the house.

Before long I'd begun to get the hang of basketball, despite being fairly clueless about tactics and the game's subtleties. My footballer's hand–eye coordination and my strength in the chair held me in good stead. In a fairly short space of time, helped by my ability to sink long-range shots, I was selected in the Australian train-on squad for the 1996 Atlanta Paralympics. This did not mean I was guaranteed to go to Atlanta, but it put me in the mix with the other likely candidates. If I trained hard and my performances were good enough I'd have every chance of being a Paralympian, something I'd never really contemplated until that point.

It was a great honour to make the squad and be in line to represent my country. Increasingly, I was enjoying my basketball and the experience of playing in curtain-raisers to Sydney Kings' games at the Sydney Entertainment Centre. But in between these thrills, my mind began to wander and I questioned whether my heart was really in it. When those feelings intensified I withdrew from the squad. (I should point out here that my absence hardly tore the heart out of the team. They went on to win gold in Atlanta and I couldn't have been happier for them.)

What sparked the doubt was that I'd begun to think again of Hawaii.

It didn't help that by this time it was early 1996 and, being school holidays, my job with Spinesafe was in a brief hiatus. So I had plenty of time to sit at home, stare out the windows and let my thoughts take flight.

What kept coming back to me was the nagging feeling that, despite all I'd achieved in completing the 1995 race, I hadn't quite done what I'd set out to do. No matter how positively I deconstructed 1995, there was no getting past that fact. By this stage my body had fully recovered from the battering it took at Kona and I was starting to forget the pain associated with training for, and undertaking, a race of that magnitude. (It's not my area of

EXECUTING A REVERSE LAY-UP DURING TRAINING FOR WHEELCHAIR BASKETBALL AT PENRITH IN 1994

expertise, but isn't that how mothers continue to have more children despite professing 'Never again!' after the searing pain of giving birth to their first child?)

In essence, the more I thought about Hawaii 1995 the more I was plagued by 'what ifs'. What if I'd done more training? What if I hadn't underestimated the course? What if I'd had a better handcycle? What if I'd gone out harder in the cycle leg while I still had the strength? What if that damn wind hadn't been blowing with cyclonic force? Of course the 'what if?' game is an exercise in futility, because the only way to answer the questions is to have another crack.

The second this crossed my mind, a new goal was born.

AS BEFORE, I WOULD HAVE TO QUALIFY for the race by getting through a preliminary event. In 1995, that was in Panama City. In 1996, it would be in Santa Rosa, California. Unlike able-bodied competitors, who had a host of races through the year that acted as qualifiers, wheelchair competitors were given just one opportunity. That increased the pressure significantly. One off day and it could all be over.

Amid my preparations, I flew to Canada to meet my extended family. My brother Don, who'd so generously supported me in Hawaii 1995, was instrumental in facilitating this meeting and I can't thank him enough. Initially, as you might expect, it was odd meeting these people with whom I shared so much genetically but knew so little about. The rapport wasn't instant and I remember greeting my sister Morag with an almost businesslike handshake.

But things happen for a reason as far as I'm concerned, and as it turned out, it was my arriving in Canada in a wheelchair that allowed Morag to open up to me in a way she may not have done otherwise. It lowered her guard. If I'd turned up exuding a sense of having had the most brilliant, carefree life, I don't think we would have made the same connection. As I had to remind myself, Morag and her siblings had suffered in their own ways after Dad left them.

Meeting Morag, Don and Kenny allowed me to finally develop an understanding of what Dad left behind when he emigrated from Scotland with Mum all those years ago. Living so far away from them, it was always hard to appreciate that Morag, Don and Kenny were as real as Marc, Marion and me. They were more like concepts than flesh and blood, and I can't say I ever gave too much thought to how they must have been affected by Dad's split with their mother, Margaret.

Morag explained to me how baffled and hurt they were by the breakdown of their parents' relationship. She told me she never had hard feelings towards me and my siblings, but all she wanted was for her father to come home. For many young girls, a father is a knight in shining armour, and Morag struggled for years with the fact that her father had abandoned her. For a long time, she managed to convince herself that he would be coming back, but eventually she had to face the confronting truth.

Over a period of a few months, I had the opportunity to grow into my Canadian family. I not only reacquainted myself with Don and met Morag and Kenny, I was also introduced to their families. I recall giving a talk at Kenny's son Devlin's school after Devlin had written and read out a beautiful essay about me in front of his class. That so impressed his teacher he was invited to read the same essay in front of the entire school, and I was there to see it. When he was done, he finished with, 'And this is my Uncle John' which was one of the most memorable introductions I've ever had before a speaking engagement.

In such a short time they made me feel welcome, and I developed a genuine sense of belonging which I hadn't expected. As a bonus, with an eye to Hawaii, I continued to train in Canada and competed in a few local triathlons to keep my hand in.

Yet again I couldn't help but think that none of this good—this connection to my family on the other side of the world—would have happened had I not been struck down by the truck. It was an uncomfortable realisation to come to, for it poses a question that is so difficult to answer. Was getting hit by the truck such a bad thing after all?

RECOVERING AT THE FINISH LINE AFTER COMPLETING THE QUALIFYING RACE—A HALF-IRONMAN
EVENT IN SANTA ROSA, CALIFORNIA—IN THE LEAD-UP TO THE 1996 HAWAIIAN IRONMAN

UNLIKE IN PANAMA CITY IN 1995, I was the only wheelchair athlete contesting the qualification race in Santa Rosa. This gave me the luxury of not having to worry at all about my time. All I had to do was finish the race, a half-Ironman event (comprising a 1.9-kilometre swim, 90-kilometre cycle and 21.1-kilometre run). Things went well for me on the day in Santa Rosa and I, ahem, 'won' the wheelchair section (congratulations, John, I hear you say, you're a champion) and qualified for Hawaii. Some prize, when you think of the torture it involves.

One of the people who came to support me in Santa Rosa was a gorgeous radiologist I had met in Panama City. By the time of the Santa Rosa race, Cynthia and I had been seeing a lot of each other and romance had blossomed. So, when I returned to Panama City from Santa Rosa, I stayed with Cynthia at her house which was, conveniently, just a few minutes' drive from the beach.

While in the evenings I reprised my role as cook for a very grateful Cynthia, by day I trained hard in the heat and the humidity to prepare myself for the rigours of Hawaii. I was memorably helped out by a bloke called Don 'Pee Wee' Bramblett who, on our training days, would come and collect me from Cynthia's place in the pre-dawn black and drive me and my equipment to a nearby military base, where he worked as a diving instructor. There I'd do laps of the base's 10-kilometre circuit alternating, on different days, between my handcycle and racing chair.

When the sun began to rise and the heat began to creep into the day, we'd come across the awesome sight of companies of Marines doing exercises: pushing themselves to exhaustion performing chin-ups and push-ups, then taking off in their platoons for long runs. And I'll never forget the thrill I felt every time I surged past them on my wheels, as they were jogging and singing. Breaking from their often funny military ditties, they'd chant 'Ohh ahh, super hero' each and every time I passed.

A week out from the race I was back in Kona. It was difficult to believe a year had passed. As had happened last time, a bunch of people made the extraordinary effort to leave their busy lives to come and offer me their help and support. One of these was my masseur, Kylie Nicholson, whom I met after the 1995 race when I was in desperate need of remedial work. She'd worked wonders for me and had offered to help me prepare for and recover from another Ironman when it happened. Along with Kylie, Cynthia flew in from Florida and my brother Don made it again from Canada.

Following the media coverage I'd attracted the previous year, I was again a subject of interest. I must confess my ego was stroked and I allowed myself to get carried away. NBC filmed a segment about me the day before the race, for which I agreed to do repeated hill climbs in my handcycle—a much lighter and faster model than the one I'd had the year before—which in retrospect wasn't the smartest or most professional thing to do.

While the previous year I was full of confidence, in 1996 I found myself on the eve of the race with an odd feeling in my gut, and I told Kylie about it. 'I don't feel right,' I said. 'I can't say exactly what's up but something is just not right.'

These doubts were forgotten when the cannon fired just after dawn the next day and I again fought through the washing-machine conditions at the start of the swim leg.

Gaining a boost of confidence after emerging from the water 2 minutes earlier than I did in 1995, I was soon flying in my handcycle (having been helped in transition by a couple of friends, Ernest Ferrel and Tim Twardzik) feeling utterly sure that I was not only going to make the cut-off but I was going to do so with some time to spare.

With 50 kilometres to go in the cycle leg, that belief was shattered by a distinctive rubbery bang. I'd blown a tyre. Ordinarily this would have been little more than an inconvenience, but out on the Queen K Highway the road and its surrounds were blisteringly hot and I wasn't about to haul myself off my handcycle and sit down on the tarmac to change the tyre. Given the lack of sensitivity in parts of my legs, it was possible I could get badly burnt without even knowing it. The only option I had was to pedal on, despite the flat tyre, to the next aid station, where I'd be afforded better conditions and some shade. The next aid station, however, was about 5 kilometres away and as every minute ticked by, as every cyclist without a flat tyre zipped past me, my anxiety increased.

TIM TWARDZIK (LEFT) AND ERNEST FERREL (RIGHT) CARRYING ME OUT OF THE WATER AND TO THE
TRANSITION ZONE IN THE 1996 HAWAIIAN IRONMAN

After a difficult slog I finally made the aid station and, on a patch of grass, changed the tyre. I couldn't say for sure but I felt the whole episode had robbed me of about 20 minutes. Long enough to leave me worried, particularly when, in a case of déjà vu, I saw the sun much lower in the sky than I wanted it to be. Trying to strike a balance between flogging myself and blowing up like an overworked engine, I took off as fast as seemed sensible, heading for the transition zone.

Before getting there I had to again conquer, in reverse, the short sharp hill I'd struggled up the year before. With that behind me I could hardly believe it when, coming through the transition zone, I was met by the race director Sharron Ackles and given the news I had dreaded. 'John, you've been disqualified. You've missed the cut-off by 15 minutes.'

After a 3.8-kilometre swim and a 180-kilometre cycle, I was only 15 minutes over. My mind was screaming out, 'You can't do this to me again!' but the clock didn't lie. I simply couldn't believe that after all my work and effort I'd missed the cut-off again. It was particularly hard to take because, at least in comparison to the year before, when it took Johnno's words to compel me to the finish line, I didn't feel spent. I was crushed with disappointment.

Then, just as happened in 1995, I was encouraged to go on. 'We'd love you to complete the course,' Sharron said. 'And there are a lot of people waiting for you at the finish line.'

So on I went, and the arbitrary cruelty of the cut-off times (designed, I realise, to ensure that people stay on pace to complete the race within a manageable time, considering the complex logistical demands surrounding an event of this magnitude) was pretty much all I could think about as I negotiated the hill out of town and then powered steadily through the marathon course, picking up runners and time as I went. However, by the time I approached the screaming crowds standing three-deep at the finishing chute, I allowed myself to forget the cut-off disaster and to again appreciate the significance of what I had done.

Crossing the line—once again having removed the Australian flag from my racing chair and grasped it in my hand—I noted my time: 14 hours and

39 minutes, 13 minutes faster than in 1995. Delighted that I'd improved, I was euphoric when a finisher's medal was slipped around my neck.

In the endorphin-charged aftermath I felt the task was done and, though sore and sorry, I slept the sleep of the deeply contented. I was well within the 17-hour race limit and here was a finisher's medal around my neck. I could tick Hawaii off my list of goals and get on with the rest of my life.

But with a new day came a new perspective. Don, who had been there to greet me warmly at the end of the race, soon pulled the rug from under my feet. 'John, you've got to give it back.'

'What are you talking about?'

'You've got to give the medal back.'

'What do you mean?' I asked, though I knew well enough, for a voice within me had been trying to make the same point.

'The people handing out medals just assumed you'd made all the cut-off times when you crossed the line. But you didn't. You didn't finish legitimately.'

Don was absolutely right.

For all Dad and Mum's difficulty in raising their children, they had instilled in us sound values and well-developed notions of right and wrong. Don's words made me admit what I'd managed to keep subdued since being awarded a medal.

That day I met Sharron Ackles at her office.

'There's been a mistake, Sharron. I need to give this back,' I said, and I placed the medal on her desk and explained the mix-up.

Sharron shocked me when she started to cry. Seeing her like that brought a tear to my eye and I could feel the poignancy of the moment.

'Surely if anyone deserves this medal it's you,' she said.

I wanted that medal so badly, but the circumstances weren't right and I told her so.

A day later, Don flew back to Canada, Cynthia returned to Florida (we'd left our relationship in a kind of limbo), and I jetted off to Australia. For the second year in a row I was returning without fulfilling my goal. It's a long flight from Honolulu to Sydney. When you've left a dream behind it can seem like a lifetime.

AS I HAD THE YEAR BEFORE, I returned from Hawaii in late October 1996 to an empty house and, once again, found myself staring out the window harbouring regret. Intellectually, I recognised the achievement in finishing the Ironman, but no matter how I rationalised it—and believe me, I tried to find an escape clause—I couldn't get around the fact that once again I'd missed the bike cut-off time and had been disqualified. That I made up considerable time on the run leg didn't change that.

I had to go back and get it right.

Having made that difficult decision, and having allowed myself enough time to recover physically from the race, I started looking for inspiration, anything to help prepare myself mentally for another assault on the course. I remember reading a book called *Bag of Jewels* by Susan Hayward that featured a quote by seventeenth-century German physicist Georg C. Lichtenberg which resonated for me during this time. It read: 'The worst thing you can possibly do is worry about what you could have done.' That said to me, 'Don't beat yourself up about getting so close in 1995 and 1996, and don't wait till you're an old man sitting in a rocking chair on your porch to wonder what might have happened had you given it another go.' It told me to go out and try again.

Another thing that struck a chord with me was the film *Dead Poets' Society*, in which Robin Williams's character, teacher John Keating, used the Latin expression *carpe diem* to inspire his students. While 'seize the day' certainly captured my imagination, I was far more impressed when he told his students to 'suck the marrow out of life'. While I'd never articulated it to myself quite like that until then, that's what I'd been trying to do since my accident. I'd been given a second chance and it would have been criminal of me to waste it by not striving to be the best I could be.

Inspiration from outside was one thing; help of a practical nature was something else. In the aftermath of the 1996 race I was invited to speak to Honolulu-based employees of Subaru about my accident and my subsequent efforts to get the best out of myself, including my efforts to tackle the Ironman. I agreed, and on the night found that my experience as a Spinesafe lecturer—a job that was still ongoing—helped settle my nerves.

I could feel that my story was having an effect on the listeners, which pleased me but also surprised me. I'd never really thought of myself as being anything special or out of the ordinary, and I still don't. But I was beginning to realise that others could find strength and inspiration in how I'd battled to overcome my life-changing accident.

After my talk, one of Subaru's managers, Dennis O'Keefe (who was originally from Sydney), suggested that when I return home I get in contact with a man called Tony Garnett who, Dennis suggested, could 'help me'. He wasn't specific about the type of help Tony might offer and it left me wondering.

Tony Garnett was a Holden car dealer in Blacktown, in Sydney's west. I took my time in calling him because I didn't want to bother him under the pretext of some vague notion of Dennis's that he could help me. But just before Christmas 1996 I was in the local shopping centre when, within 15 minutes, both my brother Don and Dennis O'Keefe called me from the other side of the world to check if I'd called Tony Garnett.

No, I told them, not yet.

Well do it, was the gist of their response.

Eventually, early in 1997, I got around to it and went to meet Tony at his dealership. He is a huge man which, I discovered, was just as well, as he has a huge heart to carry around. He asked me about myself and I gave him my history and told him about my accident, about Spinesafe, my two efforts in Hawaii and my dream to go back a third time and get it right.

When I was finished, Tony, who had been listening quietly said, 'I like you, you're a bit of a mongrel, you've got that glint in your eye. I want to give you a leg up. This is what we're going to do.' Tony then explained that he would get a group of friends together at the Parramatta Leagues Club and I would 'speak for my supper'. 'And let's just see what comes from that,' he concluded.

When the day arrived I went to the club with a knot in my stomach, feeling as green as they come. Tony had gathered together some of the state's biggest business and media names and they were there to hear me talk and, perhaps, decide to help me out. Supported by slides, an overhead

projector and video clips from NBC's feature on the 1995 Ironman, I spoke
about my life and my struggles to get back into the game. It's safe to say my
talk was warmly received, and when I went back to my seat I found
numerous people approaching me and putting business cards on the table
in front of me. Tony, beaming, said he'd be my secretary and manage all the
cards for me, but not before giving me a word of advice. 'Whatever you do,
don't change. Don't become too polished, don't try and be a comedian. Just
be who you are.'

Talk about people appearing in my life at the right time.

In effect, Tony launched my professional career that day—both as an
athlete and a speaker. Through his selfless mentorship and the friendship
we began to develop, I became more active in selling myself, so that as the
1997 Ironman approached, I was picking up generous sponsorship deals,
including one with Holden. Moreover, Tony ushered me from speaking for
Spinesafe at schools to speaking to people who ran their own companies, a
group I'd never thought would be interested in what I might have to say.

ALL THIS MADE AN ENORMOUS DIFFERENCE to my preparation for
Hawaii 1997, as I was able to afford to become a full-time athlete. As such,
I left Spinesafe, which had been so good to me and so good *for* me. Doing
this allowed me to structure my days around my training and devote more
time to researching things I'd always neglected, like diet and nutrition.

Being a professional also allowed me the luxury of attending more
races overseas. One such race was in St Petersburg, Florida, which was
most memorable for the fact that I again found myself meeting wonderful
people, including Jason Howard and Lee Hutchinson, a pair of Englishmen
who invited me to a barbecue one evening after training. There I met the
evening's hosts, Karen and Robert Hoke.

Once Karen and Robert heard my story and discovered I was training
to do Hawaii for the third time, they made an extremely generous offer
to put me up at their house. I stayed there six months. In this happy
home environment I had the best preparation possible for Hawaii and, as

insufficient as it was in comparison with what they'd done for me, I thanked them by getting a limousine to pick us up and take us out to a beautiful restaurant in nearby Tampa.

Living in St Petersburg also put me back in contact with Chris Peterson, the handcycle designer who'd custom-made my racing chair in 1995. Clearly my problem in both 1995 and 1996 had been the cycle leg, and I tried to give myself the best chance in 1997 by ensuring my handcycle was, like my racing chair, as good as it could be. The one he built for me was more aerodynamic, weighed just 9 kilograms and was a thing of beauty.

Once again there was a qualifying race to get through, this time a half-Ironman event in Lubbock, Texas. By now, wheelchair athletes were beginning to become more prominent in triathlon and there were to be six wheelchair athletes contesting the Lubbock race, with the first three qualifying for Hawaii. Another difference in 1997 was that the wheelchair category for Hawaii was made official, as opposed to previous years when it was described as a demonstration event. This introduced a new element. Before I was simply racing myself and the cut-off times. Now, if I managed to qualify, I would be racing myself, the cut-off times and two other athletes.

Thankfully, I qualified for Hawaii, finishing second in the Lubbock race to a guy called Scott McNeice from St Petersburg, Florida. The thrill of the former overshadowed the slight dent to my pride caused by the latter and I went to Hawaii recharged. Losing that qualifying race to Scott gave me extra motivation because it made me feel that my dream could be taken away from me.

As usual, I was lucky enough to have with me in Hawaii a bunch of people who meant the world to me. In 1997 I flew my Dad over for his 70th birthday and I also bought a flight for Michelle, with whom I'd remained friends after our separation. She had given me so much that it meant a lot to me to have her be a part of what I saw as the pinnacle of my sporting career. And I suppose I was also thinking that by having her witness the whole spectacle and what it meant to me it might, in some way, explain the desire that was in my belly when we were married and how distracted I had been by that.

For the third year in succession my brother Don flew in from Canada and he proved, as usual, a comforting presence and a reliable manager, handling all the small details I didn't want to have to think about.

Unlike 1995 and 1996, I noticed a change in my approach to the race in 1997. Understandably, I knew the course very well by now and I was careful not to get caught up in the buzz that surrounds the event. I was now a professional athlete and I adopted a professional attitude. As such, I'd arrived in Hawaii two weeks early and trained as much as possible on the course.

Dad was, by now, my biggest fan. Much to my embarrassment, he was always boasting about my achievements to anyone who'd make eye contact with him. And more than once I caught Dad pinching racing photos of me, and other competition paraphernalia, from my house so he could stick them on his wall at home in Culburra.

He was thrilled to be with me in Hawaii and, I must say, his presence was invaluable. In the evenings he'd give me therapeutic massages, and by day he'd accompany me while I was training on the Queen K either in my racing chair or new handcycle. The vehicle that Subaru had supplied had been set up with an orange light on the roof, which would flash as Dad trailed me across the lava fields, warning cars of my presence. The last thing I needed was another up close and personal with a motor vehicle.

A week out from the race everything was in place and I felt confident. Unlike my feeling of foreboding in the previous year, in 1997 I just believed it was my time.

When the race finally got underway, the early signs were good. I completed the swim in 1 hour, my best swim time yet, and set off for the bike leg feeling strong. Despite the mass of bodies on bicycles, I knew I was in front of the two other wheelchair athletes as I rounded the halfway mark and began retracing the bicycle route. This was confirmed when, heading back, I crossed paths with Scott McNeice and Randy Caddell, who were trailing me in second and third places, respectively.

They are both great athletes and seeing them spurred me on. While my main goal was to do what I hadn't yet managed to do—finish the race within all the cut-off times—I now had the added pressure of actually winning my category. To achieve one without the other would have felt insufficient; I thought of this on the return leg on my handcycle and it helped me push through the pain and fatigue. I flooded my mind with positive affirmations, leaving no room for self-doubt. 'You've worked hard for this', I stressed to myself. 'You can't let someone take it away from you. Stay strong.'

With the end of the cycle leg in my sights I knew that finally, after three attempts, I was going to make the cut-off time. It was an enormous relief but not one I wallowed in, simply because there was still 42.2 kilometres to travel and I was no longer just racing myself and the clock. So I pushed through the transition and past the points where in previous years officials had informed me of my disqualification.

WITH MY FATHER, ALEX, AND BROTHER DON AT OUR KONA HOTEL IN THE DAYS LEADING UP TO THE 1997 HAWAIIAN IRONMAN

MY SWISH NEW HANDCYCLE MADE ALL THE DIFFERENCE IN THE 1997 HAWAIIAN IRONMAN

The marathon started well and there was no sign of Scott or Randy. I'd regularly been drinking water and eating carbohydrate gels, but early on I ran out of my own supplies and, somewhat reluctantly, had to use an energy drink I hadn't sampled much before. For whatever reason it didn't agree with me and over the next 20 kilometres I vomited six times, feeling my energy levels drop after each episode.

But, despite my upset stomach, I managed to keep my speed up and keep Scott and Randy off my tail. When I saw the lights of Kona looming I knew I had it. The feeling was incredible.

Once again I had the luxury of coasting down the final straight and soaking up the atmosphere and well wishes of the spectators who draped themselves over the barricades. And when I crossed that line (in 12 hours and 21 minutes), as the winner of my category, I crossed it knowing that I hadn't done it alone. Without Johnno, David, Don, Marion, Dad, Michelle and a host of others I wouldn't have got even close. I didn't see it as *my* victory so much as *our* victory.

On a more personal level, the pleasure of finishing that race was heightened by all the pain and suffering I'd endured. And I think in some ways it meant more to me knowing it took me three attempts to do it. While I'd been an accomplished athlete I'd never been exceptional. So knowing I had persevered through some low moments to finally achieve what I set out to do made it all the more special.

We can't always get the things we want the first time around.

IRONMAN

KAILUA-KONA, HAWAII
OCTOBER 18, 1997

4 MILE
SWIM

112 MILE
BIKE

26.2 MILE
RUN

902

AFTER TWO FAILED ATTEMPTS, AND MUCH HEARTACHE, AN IRONMAN FINISHER'S MEDAL
FINALLY LAY AROUND MY NECK IN THIS OFFICIAL PHOTOGRAPH

_09

09 THROWING MYSELF IN THE DEEP END

PART OF ME ALWAYS THOUGHT Michelle and I would get back together. She and I had known each other for so long, and she had stuck by me so faithfully through my darkest days, that it almost seemed wrong that we could somehow end up with other people. To the romantic in me it seemed we were due a fairytale ending.

After she came to support me in Hawaii there was a flicker of reconciliation in the air and in the week leading up to the race, when I think Michelle got an insight into the type of life I wanted, we greatly enjoyed each other's company. The sense of being on holiday—or at least being away from the reality of home—allowed us to relax, and we knew each other so well there was a kind of comfort in it.

But once we were home again reality closed in around us. We saw each other a few times in beautifully romantic settings, willing to see what might happen, but each time I couldn't block out the voice within telling me that nothing had changed. It wasn't just that we had different ideas for a future together (I was by now totally addicted to the endorphins sport served up in huge doses), but that the missing ingredient in our relationship was just not going to appear, as much as I wanted it to. The fairytale just wasn't to be.

IF THE VOICE WITHIN TOLD ME THERE WAS NO FUTURE for Michelle and me, it also told me categorically that I would never again have the desire to put myself through more pain on the lava fields of Kona. I'd finally done what I had set out to do.

Of course, the completion of a goal, however long standing, is so often accompanied by a sense of anticlimax and what feels like a void. Some call it the 'Ironman Blues', but you could just as easily refer to it as the 'now what?' moment.

Having always had a busy nature, I've never enjoyed the lull that follows a high. Basking in the glory of a completed goal is all well and good but, for me at least, the pleasure is more in the journey than the destination. So, even before finishing Hawaii 1997, I'd pencilled in a new challenge, and it was soon after recovering at home that I decided to go ahead with it.

I wanted to swim the English Channel.

Growing up in a country with a proud history of distance swimming, I'd long been aware of the exploits of Des Renford and Susie Maroney, but I'd never contemplated that kind of a swim myself until, swimming laps in the summer of 1995, I bumped into Ian Byrne, a Sydney solicitor who, months earlier, had swum the Channel. Ian and I recognised each other from articles in the local paper and he came over to congratulate me on finishing Hawaii. Similarly, I praised his efforts and he gave me an overview of his Channel swim, which impressed me greatly and I said as much.

'Well,' he replied, 'if I can do it, you can do it.'

I'm sure he didn't mean it as some kind of challenge (although Ian later made the comment that I 'took the bait') but with that throwaway line Ian sowed an idea that, even during the following two years when I was engaged in further Hawaiian odysseys, never left my mind. In fact, early on in my preparations for the 1997 Hawaiian Ironman, I began reading up on the English Channel, principally to find out what it would take to make a successful crossing. As part of my reading, I discovered that the first Australian to swim the Channel was Sydneysider Linda McGill, a former Commonwealth Games and Olympic swimmer, who did it in August 1965. McGill would complete the feat twice more.

To get a more comprehensive picture, I decided to complement my reading with first-hand knowledge. Through a mutual acquaintance, I contacted Des Renford, who was in his late sixties at the time. Des hadn't so much swum the Channel as had a relationship with it. Known for good reason as the 'King of the Channel' and the 'Calais commuter', Des swam the famous stretch of water an incredible nineteen times between 1970 and 1980, his first time being an attempt at a double crossing when he was 42. Though he didn't quite make it there and back, that first swim typified Des's courage. Within sight of Dover on the return leg, a huge wave picked him up and smashed him against the hull of his support vessel. Despite dislocating his shoulder, Des ploughed on until his support team was forced to pull him out of the water.

Turning up at Des's place in Sydney's Maroubra with David Wells in tow, I listened, fascinated, as this rugged man with a broad weathered smile recounted details of his many crossings and warned me of the difficulties and dangers of the busy waterway, which is about 32 kilometres across at the shortest point. But swimmers never take a straight line, as their pilot-boat captains look to make the most of the conditions. Depending on tides and weather the distance actually covered by a Channel swimmer can be considerably greater, as much as double.

Hearing me outline my intentions and speak a little about my sporting background, Des said he was impressed with what I'd done but he wasn't convinced I knew exactly what I was in for.

'The Channel is an amazing body of water,' he said, sitting in his home office, which contained sea charts, maps of the Channel and a scale replica of the *Helen Ann Marie*, the support boat that accompanied him on many of his crossings. 'One minute it can be as flat as a carpet, the next it can be sending in 20-foot [6-metre] waves.'

He also set me straight on my plan to do 'the old ditch' in a wetsuit, which he pointed out wasn't allowed under the rules of the England-based Channel Swimming Association (CSA), which oversees Channel-crossing attempts. If a swim was to be considered official, one of the rules stipulated that the swimmer could only wear a bathing suit, a swimming cap, goggles and, if desired, grease or fat smeared over the body to aid heat retention in the often frigid waters. But no wetsuit. Considering my legs are nothing but dead weight in the water, this would add a considerable amount of difficulty to my attempt, notwithstanding the fact that salt water aids buoyancy.

After we'd spent a few hours together, Des expressed his support and suggested a time of year (the English late summer) in which the Channel would be at its most benign. He also promised to hook me up with an experienced boat captain by the name of Reg Brickell. Reg had overseen many successful Channel swims and, showing his pedigree, was the son of Reg Brickell Snr, who had guided Des on many of his crossings. It was lovely of Des to help me out in this way and nicer still when he and his wife, Patty, took David and me out to dinner at a local Italian restaurant.

With Des's blessing I was even more determined to take on the Channel and I went back to the books to find out all I could. As I'd discover, the first man to swim the Channel was Captain Matthew Webb, who breaststroked across on 25 August 1875 (coincidentally, 25 August was Des Renford's birthday). Taking a route from Dover, England, to Calais, France, Captain Webb completed his pioneering achievement in a time of 21 hours and 45 minutes, stopping along the way to sip on hot tea and eat a little beef as he bobbed in the water. At the time, the Mayor of Dover predicted: 'Never in the history of the world will any such feat be performed by anyone else.'

The Mayor has since been proved wrong by some 640 swimmers, but that isn't all that many people in 130 years. To put it into perspective, there have been more than 1400 ascents of Mt Everest since 1953. As this suggests, the Channel can be forbidding and is a formidable test of resolve. Legendary US swimming coach James 'Doc' Counsilman—who, in 1979, aged 58, became the oldest man to swim the Channel—summed it up succinctly when he said, 'It only hurt once; from beginning to end'.

Perhaps the clincher for me, despite everything that pointed to the difficulty of the challenge, was discovering that no wheelchair athlete had ever done it. Nor had anyone, physically challenged or otherwise, conquered both the Channel and the Hawaiian Ironman. The opportunity to break new ground appealed to me. Certainly it appealed to my ego, but I think it also had much to do with my continuing determination to prove myself as capable as anyone—and, by association, to prove that people confined to wheelchairs are not the helpless souls some believe.

I wanted my swim to be official, so I wrote to the CSA seeking permission to swim the Channel. Permission would grant me an observer and a place in the record books should I get across. In response, the CSA set up a subcommittee to decide whether they'd allow me to attempt what they called a 'special swim'. Safety, I understand, was one of their primary concerns—I don't think they wanted my death on their hands should the challenge prove too difficult. It was not an entirely unfounded fear, since six swimmers are known to have died attempting the crossing.

Eventually it came down to a vote, and while two of the CSA's five-person panel said no, three approved the swim. I was angry that anyone, even if they were in the minority, would try to deny me an opportunity to do something simply because I was a paraplegic. But I didn't dwell on it for too long because I now had my goal approved. Proving the doubters wrong would be an added bonus.

IT WAS ABOUT THIS TIME THAT I GOT TO KNOW DAVID KNIGHT, then managing director of the Australian arm of Gatorade, which had become one of my sponsors. I'd first met David in 1996 when I was competing in a triathlon at Noosa Heads, on the Queensland Sunshine Coast. Gatorade was one of the race's sponsors and David had just moved to the company from snack-food manufacturer Frito-Lay, where he had been working for eleven years. As David would admit himself, he had probably indulged in his former company's product a little too often and, at 130 kilograms with a 112-centimetre waist, he was about as far from an athlete as one could be.

Gatorade's marketing team had set up a number of dinners so David could meet some of the leading athletes in the Noosa race. David recalls seeing me at this dinner and being struck by my 'self-confidence and focus'. He also says I was dressed in black, had a shaved head and a Nike earring and, most worrying of all, was wearing sunglasses, despite the function being at night. In my defence, my recollection is that the dinner was actually lunch, which would at least explain the sunglasses.

It was a year before I met David again. Soon after I returned from finally conquering Hawaii in 1997, I saw him sitting on the steps of the Sydney Opera House with his wife, Andrea, and his children, watching the start of an International Triathlon Union event designed to road test the proposed 2000 Olympic triathlon course. I remembered him and reintroduced myself. Immediately, David says, he was struck by how different I seemed, and not only because I was wearing jeans and a T-shirt and had allowed my hair to grow back to its normal state of unruly blond curls. He says I was all smiles and more relaxed than he remembered, and I suppose this had a lot to do with the peace I'd found within myself.

We immediately struck up a rapport. I liked David, and his positive character, immensely. During our conversation, he told me how meeting me in Noosa had inspired him to lose some weight and begin training for the 1997 Noosa Triathlon, which was coming up in a week's time. We only spoke for an hour on that occasion, but before we parted I had committed to go to Noosa and do the race with him. We spent the best part of a week together in Noosa, training and getting to know each other, and it was obvious to me that David and I were forming a strong friendship. When he managed to finish the race I was very proud of him; it demonstrated his strength of mind that he had turned things around in so short a time.

That night, we celebrated at the after-party where all the elite athletes and sponsors get together to unwind. Having finished his first triathlon and proved something to himself, David was on a high, and I remember him coming over to me on the edge of the throbbing dance floor. He and I got talking (David recalls that he was sitting on the floor with his elbows on my knees) and we found ourselves sharing intimate details of our lives, such as stories about our childhoods, our inner feelings and motivations in life. And at the end of it, we decided to set each other some challenges.

I began by asking David what he was going to do next, now that he'd done his first triathlon. He deflected my question, obviously buying himself time, by asking me what I wanted to do. It was then I told him my desire to be the first wheelchair athlete to swim the English Channel. David seemed pretty impressed by that. Perhaps the bourbon he was drinking had something to do with it, but he then announced his next challenge was to do an Ironman.

Earlier, I had tried to convince him that this was something he really could achieve. Using myself as an example, I told him that my success was not simply a result of my being athletic. A race like Hawaii is about mind over body and if someone wanted to do it badly enough, and was willing to put in the work, they could. I was thrilled that he'd taken up the idea.

We made a pact to help each other out with these challenges, and David also suggested that Gatorade might be able to help me in my Channel quest.

Within a week I found myself in the company's Australian headquarters in Sydney, armed with a rudimentary presentation that I hoped would help my cause. I had prepared a biography of myself and, having already given a number of spirited but still somewhat amateurish motivational talks, I was all set to do the same again. But as I faced the dozen or so Gatorade executives, I decided, on the spur of the moment, to divert from my rehearsed speech and simply speak from the heart.

'I'd love you to support me because I want to get exposure for kids in wheelchairs,' I began. 'I'm not here for any money for myself, I just want children in wheelchairs to see that their life isn't as limited as they may think it is. If I'd become a paraplegic as a child, or was born with spina bifida, I think I'd be looking for inspiration, too. Maybe if you help me do this they will get some inspiration from me.'

After my involvement in Spinesafe and the Ironman, I had taken it upon myself to be a flag-bearer for kids in wheelchairs around the world. I was particularly conscious of showing them that, given a good dose of determination, they could do a lot more than they might believe in their darker moments. However, that brief speech was, I think, the first time I'd articulated my shifting priorities. I can't pretend my attempts at conquering Hawaii were about anyone other than myself, and my family and friends who'd supported me. Having something to prove to myself had been my overwhelming motivation. But in the lead-up to the Channel swim I was slowly beginning to lose some of my self-obsession and see a broader picture. I've no doubt that this is because I was feeling more comfortable in my own skin. Finishing Hawaii showed me that I didn't have as much to prove to myself anymore. I was growing and gradually realising that there was more to life than John Maclean and his need for affirmation.

Straight after I told the Gatorade executives I wasn't there for any personal gain, David stood up, thanked me for coming and ended the meeting. Initially, I thought I'd said the wrong thing for it all to conclude so abruptly. But David rushed out to me as I was heading to the elevator and managed to get his hand in just before the door closed. Then he looked me in the eye. 'John, you'll never know how much we just got out of what you said. You'll never know,' he told me.

I continued down to the ground floor wondering what on earth it was I had actually said.

A few weeks later I'd agreed to speak at a Gatorade conference in Bowral, a picturesque country town in the highlands some 100 kilometres south-west of Sydney. The company put me up for the night at a lovely hotel and, in return, I showed some slides and gave a talk about my struggles, concentrating on the themes of perseverance and commitment. It seemed to hit the right notes.

The next morning, David thanked me again and asked me to send him an invoice for my troubles. I had no idea what I should charge for that sort of thing and I explained to him that being put up at a nice hotel, given a meal and having the opportunity to meet more of his crew was payment enough. If all this helped me get their support to publicise the abilities of wheelchair athletes then that was enough for me. It felt the right thing to do.

Through all of this, David and I grew ever closer. It's encouraging to know that no matter how old you are, opportunities are always there to make new connections with people who will completely change and enrich your life. You just have to be open enough to let that happen.

I'VE NEVER BEEN ONE TO KEEP MY GOALS CLOSE TO MY CHEST. Sometimes I think people who do that are afraid of making their intentions known just in case they fail. For me, knowing that many people are aware of the challenge I've set myself helps me stay motivated. So, inevitably, my intention to swim the Channel made it into the local paper. Reading that story prompted Ian Morgan, from the Sydney suburb of St Clair, to offer his services as a training partner. Ian had been a fitness fanatic for many years and he said if he could help me in any way I only had to ask.

Ian's appearance on the scene was well timed. This was a period in my life when many of my stalwart friends, like Johnno and David Wells, weren't as available as before. While I was jumping in and out of relationships with abandon (including many that aren't worth going into here), they were settling down with their partners and starting families. They were as supportive of my goals as ever, but they just didn't have the time to help me train.

So when I was granted permission to swim at the Penrith Lakes complex as long as I had someone to assist me (the Lakes was being upgraded to become the Sydney International Regatta Centre with the 2000 Sydney Olympics in mind), I quickly took Ian up on his offer. I'd trained at the Lakes with Ched Towns numerous times during our swimming days and I felt very much at home there. Obviously I was not keen on getting mown down by a boat crew in full cry, so our plan was that Ian would paddle along beside me on a wave ski.

As the weeks and months flew by, I threw myself into my training with Ian and would catch up with David Knight on weekends. With David's help, Gatorade had agreed to support me for my Channel swim. Not only would they help financially, they announced they would also fund a documentary of my swim. For all the interest I knew I'd get from newspapers and television media this seemed like a particularly good idea and I envisaged the potential reach of a well-made documentary.

Around this time I reconnected with a bloke called Wally Brumniach, a triathlete whom I'd first met at the Byron Bay Blues Festival in 1996. He had introduced himself and we had an instant chemistry. It wouldn't be an overstatement to say that Wally, who was a few years older than me, quickly became a mentor. I greatly admired his outlook on life. Wally, who worked for a life coach called Maurie Raynor, was the first person to ever suggest to me that all the answers to our questions lie within, if only we'd take the time to look. As this suggests, Wally is not a bloke who avoids the tough questions and, while it took some getting used to, he constantly challenged me—and still does—to speak from the heart.

Considering all this, I was delighted when Wally volunteered his services as a support swimmer for my Channel bid. Hot on his heels was David Knight. CSA regulations state that after the first two hours, a Channel swimmer is allowed the company of a support swimmer for every alternate hour afterwards. This meant that after the first two hours of my swim had elapsed, Wally would jump in and swim with me for an hour, before leaving me for an hour on my own. Then David would join me for an hour before I had another hour solo. And so on until, hopefully, I hauled myself onto dry sand at Calais.

For David, this was more than a business obligation. Gatorade isn't so cruel that it would demand its employees take a bullet for the company. It was just something he wanted to do for himself, and out of solidarity for me. It was an enormous physical challenge for him and I was incredibly touched by his offer.

The momentum was gathering.

A FEW MONTHS AFTER I RETURNED HOME from Hawaii 1997, I played host to Jason Howard and Lee Hutchinson, the two English blokes who'd introduced me to Karen and Robert Hoke, my hosts in St Petersburg, Florida. Jason and Lee spent four months at my place and they joined my Channel training team for the first half of 1998. As I'd already discovered, it's so much easier to push yourself in a training regime if you have a committed training partner. Over the years I've become so used to (and indebted to) the support and camaraderie of others while training that now I find it nearly impossible to motivate myself to train alone.

With Jason and Lee joining Ian, Wally and David Knight, I had plenty of partners to keep me motivated and keep my eyes on the goal of crossing the Channel. Initially, I was simply clocking up the kilometres across the Lakes, but as the weather turned cooler, I knew I had to take drastic measures to enable me to cope with the cold I could face in the Channel.

At 80 kilograms, I didn't feel especially inured to the cold and, what with all the training I was doing, I was finding it difficult to put on weight. Sports dietitian Dr Helen O'Connor confirmed the importance of this.

'I don't know what you think you're in for, John, but if you don't put on weight, and a lot of it, you're wasting your time. You'll go hypothermic and you'll have no chance of completing the crossing.'

'How much weight do I need to put on?' I asked.

'Twenty kilos should do it.'

I couldn't believe it. By this stage I was swimming some 10 kilometres a day. How was I going to put on 20 kilos—a quarter of my body weight?

The diet Dr O'Connor gave me showed me how.

On waking up, I would consume five or six pieces of toast with honey or jam. That was washed down with a glass of orange juice. After that, I would hit the water and swim 10 kilometres, during which time I'd keep my energy up with a carbohydrate gel and Gatorade. Then I'd have breakfast — a protein shake, a dozen Weet-bix, a litre of milk and half a can of fruit. For good measure I'd then have another four or five pieces of toast.

Morning tea was scheduled for about 11am, during which time I'd consume a couple of coffees which helped wash down a few slices of cake. Then I'd polish things off with a rum and raisin thickshake. For lunch I'd indulge in the fatty delights of sausage rolls and pies. After giving that a few hours to sit, I'd have afternoon tea, which was essentially more cake.

Around 3pm I'd do another 3 to 5 kilometres of swimming, before having an early dinner consisting of enormous quantities of rice, chicken and vegetables. The coup de grâce was a family-size block of chocolate.

The result of this massive consumption (which I have to say wasn't difficult to ingest since my daily schedule of 15 kilometres in the water made me ravenous) was the weight gain I needed. Every day I bulked up, and within a mere four months I was pushing the scales at 100 kilograms, a full 20 kilograms heavier.

Having been fit, muscled and lean for as long as I could remember, I had some difficulty adjusting to my new look and if it wasn't for the greater good it would certainly have affected my self-esteem. But I needed to do it. Though Ian made a habit of telling me it was always a few degrees warmer than it was, the water temperature at the Lakes dropped to 9 degrees Celsius in winter. On such days, when my early-morning breath left my body in plumes of steam, I was grateful for the extra insulation. It hardly made me warm in the water, but I could certainly feel the difference in my comfort level once I got over the initial shock.

The seven months I spent in intensive training leading up to the Channel swim were both immensely enjoyable and physically trying. For one thing, physiotherapist Oliver Weber had to give me weekly treatment on my left shoulder. In Hawaii 1995 I'd suffered a partial tear to my rotator cuff tendon and it needed constant monitoring. Besides the shoulder niggle, it wasn't always easy getting up at first light and, before the sun had a chance to get rid of the night's thin frost, to drop into the Lakes. However, what I did enjoy was working towards a goal, feeling myself getting stronger and more determined. And there was the company of my training team.

Not that they were always happy with me, especially Jason and Lee. As part of my plan to acclimatise, I decided to leave off the indoor heating in winter. Australia, generally speaking, is a warm, dry continent, but there are plenty of places that get brass-monkey cold in winter. While snow in Australia is pretty much confined to the imaginatively named Snowy Mountains near the New South Wales–Victoria border, at night in Penrith temperatures can drop to near zero, so I wasn't too popular with Jason and Lee, who always had to rug up inside like Antarctic explorers.

Nor did they appreciate my method of getting them out of bed for these morning swims. It involved me routinely putting on the soundtrack of *The*

TRAINING AT PENRITH LAKES WITH IAN MORGAN (ON THE WAVE SKI) AND FLATMATE JASON HOWARD (RIGHT)

Blues Brothers and cranking the volume right up. My chosen track was always 'The Old Landmark' by James Brown, which featured the appropriate line, 'You've got to wake up!'.

To build up to distances or swimming times resembling those of the Channel crossing, we'd scheduled a progressive series of swims, beginning with a 4-hour effort and working up to 8-, 10- and, finally, 12-hour swims.

By this stage, David Harvey, a respected swim coach, had seen me ploughing furrows into the Penrith pool one day and, after a long conversation about my goals (he did a double take when I told him I was going to swim the Channel), offered to become my coach. He was there coaching me when I did my first 4-hour swim—a comfortable effort it turned out to be—at the Lakes in the late afternoon. Also there were David Knight and Wally (who had flown down from Queensland), themselves in training for the important roles they would play when it came time for me to crawl across the Channel. This team was together again when, from Cronulla beach, in Sydney's south, Wally, David, Jason and I set off for a 6-hour swim (overseen by David Harvey in a boat), memorable for the painful jellyfish stings I suffered on my arms. Jellyfish may be small but their floss-thin tentacles can pack a wallop—as I'd discovered on that Botany Bay beach with my brother Marc all those years ago.

Perhaps the most memorable of these training swims was a 10-hour swim we did on the Shoalhaven River, about 160 kilometres south of Sydney and close to Dad and Mum's place. While the swim was set up purely for training purposes, it differed from my previous efforts in that the documentary crew was aboard to get some early footage.

We started around 10am and were fortunate to have the use of two boats. One, a recreational vessel owned and piloted by a friend, Ken Smith, carried David Harvey, and it cruised along beside me and Wally, who was supporting me in the water. David needed to be that close to monitor my stroke rating (that is, count my strokes per minute to ensure I wasn't going faster, or slower, than my optimum rate), my style and, every now and then, take blood from me to test my blood-sugar levels. The other boat was a fishing vessel that carried the documentary crew and Dad.

Later in the afternoon, however, the fishing boat had to leave us, so everyone piled into Ken's boat, which wasn't really designed for so many passengers. Nevertheless, it motored along beside me as the swim continued through the afternoon and into the night.

Hour after hour, Wally was tremendous. Aside from tackling the whole of the lengthy swim himself, he regularly offered me encouragement. Swimming, obviously, isn't conducive to conversation, so the encouragement was often simply a whoop, a holler, or a 'Good on you, mate, you're doing well'. It doesn't sound like much but it makes the world of difference. Never once did I consider I was tackling the Channel on my own. This was a team effort.

But some 8 hours into the swim, I noticed that Wally was getting rather quiet. He hadn't said anything to me since our last break, about a half hour earlier. I paused to look at him properly in the dim light. He was pale and not looking entirely comfortable. The next time I slowed my stroke to turn to him I saw he was up in the boat, wrapped in a blanket and sipping tea. He was hypothermic. Normally, in such a state, you'd be laid out on your back and told to conserve your energy. But Wally was sitting up, and though he was shaking and chattering like a maraca, he was still clapping and offering me encouragement. 'You're doing it, mate, you're doing it,' he said, and I felt a bolt of energy and resolve shoot through me. This small incident epitomised the sacrifices all these people were making to help me—it was humbling and energising at the same time.

A few hours later I broke from the reverie of the long-distance swimmer—a kind of meditative state where your brain feels largely switched off for hours at a time—to see that the boat was no longer puttering beside me and I was swimming in complete darkness. I could see on one of the banks the milky glow of a lonely streetlight, but it seemed pointless heading towards it, since I could hardly get out and walk home. So I just kept going, figuring they knew what they were doing.

Back on the boat, meantime, Dad was frantic because they'd lost sight of me. But the boat was in danger of breaking down. The spotlights they'd had trained on me had begun to seriously suck the battery. The pace I was setting meant the battery was being drained at a faster rate than it was being charged. Seeing this, Ken had to let me go on while they ran the boat in fast circles to try to recharge the battery.

I missed all the tension of this as I stroked happily enough through the oil-black skin of the river. I'm not one to let my imagination run away with me, so I enjoyed the odd sensation of swimming in the dark, never once thinking about what might have been slithering around in the water beneath me. Eventually the boat was sufficiently charged and they raced after me, being careful not to run me down.

I'd been in the water almost 10 hours when they found me and everyone agreed, after that little drama, that it was time to call it a day. Or a night. I was soon in the boat, wrapped up like a Christmas ham, eating rice pudding and thinking what a success the day had been.

By the close of the seventh month of training—just before we headed to England in early August 1998—I'd brought my stroke rate down from 80 a minute to 60 without sacrificing any speed (thus expending less effort for the same result). And in total I'd swum some 1800 kilometres, which is about the distance up Australia's east coat from Melbourne to Brisbane.

To think, ten years earlier I had emerged from my first session in the hydrotherapy pool at Royal North Shore Hospital exhausted after swimming two strokes.

10

ENGLAND TO FRANCE—
THE HARD WAY

FROM THE WINDSWEPT TOP of the White Cliffs of Dover, the English Channel looks immense. Only on the clearest days, when the salt spray is calmed and the smudge of haze has lifted, is the coast of France visible. In between lies a rolling mass of water, its uniformity broken only by thousands of whitecaps and an incredible number of watercraft. The Channel is one of the world's busiest shipping lanes and some 1200 vessels use it daily. I've heard it said that swimming the Channel can be like crossing a busy highway.

Seeing it from this vantage point (and an even higher one when, on another day, David Knight and I took a helicopter ride around the cliffs), the magnitude of the challenge was very real. It felt like an intimidating physical presence in our midst. Nevertheless, I was confident. Despite my shoulder injury, I'd done the training, I'd swum in water colder than the Channel would be in August, and I had assembled a great team around me. The only things that could defeat me were the elements. The wind and tide would need to be kind.

I'd heard of people training for months, even years, to make their crossing, only to find the weather against them on the day. I can imagine their distress when their crossing attempt ended before they'd even got wet. Others had come within a kilometre or less of France only to find a shifting tide barring their way as effectively as a brick wall. That is, a brick wall that actually advances on you, forcing you backwards and, inevitably, out of the water and back into your pilot boat. So close and yet so far.

Ultimately, the decision of when I was to swim would come down to Reg Brickell, skipper of my pilot boat, *The Viking Princess*. Reg would have to match up a free day in his busy schedule (Reg and his brother Ray were fishermen and had other swimmers to guide across the Channel that summer) with a day when the forecast predicted favourable weather.

Shortly after arriving in England, we met the brothers at a pub in Folkestone. They were a salty pair of characters, forever in blue singlets, no matter the weather. They weren't exactly garrulous—we had to buy them a pint to prise their lips apart—but when they got talking it was clear they knew the Channel like a farmer knows his fields. Although we'd spoken on the phone and tentatively lined up 14 August as the day of my swim, Reg told me I couldn't count on it since the weather was fickle and I was in a queue. So it became a waiting game.

Waiting at least allowed us to familiarise ourselves with the area, to get in 4- to 5-kilometre daily swims around the cliffs, and meet a few of the local inhabitants, such as Les Kennett. An old bloke who could have walked straight out of the pages of *Moby-Dick*, Les regaled us with stories of guiding swimmers across the Channel by rowboat. Setting off before dawn, the swimmers only knew where they were going by following the red glow from Les's ever-lit cigarette. When we asked him why so many people want to swim the Channel, his answer was straight to the point: 'Because it's bloody difficult.'

My team based itself in Deal, Kent, in a holiday village that time forgot. So drowsy and antiquated was it, you had to feed a meter to keep up supplies of hot water and heating. But despite the somewhat decrepit state of the place, we kept ourselves entertained and busy.

AT A BEACH NEAR DOVER IN 1998, CONTEMPLATING THE MAGNITUDE OF THE CHANNEL
CROSSING A WEEK BEFORE MY FIRST ATTEMPT

There was a big crew on hand to support me. David Knight, Wally and David Harvey were there. So was Wally's wife, Natalie; Marion; Don and his kids Megan and Sean; a photographer friend, Lisa Saad; George Lawlor from Nike; Cynthia (who flew in from Florida to lend her support); and the documentary crew.

The film crew wanted me to start my attempt every bit as much as I did, given that I couldn't offer them much in the lead-up other than telling them how excited I was. Not exactly riveting stuff. I was hoping my swimming would give them all the material they needed.

Finally a call came through from Reg to say that on 17 August I would have my crack at the Channel.

WHEN THE DAY FINALLY ARRIVED, I found myself maintaining an uneasy balance of excitement and nerves. I sat quietly aboard *The Viking Princess* as it took us from the fishing docks at Folkestone to the starting point of the swim, the shore under Shakespeare Cliff, about a half-hour boat ride away. We chugged through the morning in Reg's fishing boat as David Harvey smeared me in wool fat, thick, viscous and white, not unlike zinc cream in its consistency. While the water was 16 degrees, balmy compared to the Lakes in winter, it would seem much colder after I'd been in for a few hours and I hoped the wool fat would help.

Apart from Don's kids, Lisa Saad and Cynthia, everyone in my team was able to fit on the boat, along with an official observer from the CSA whose name befitted his position: Norm Trusty. Seeing everyone aboard just made me more anxious to get started. Let's go to work, I thought, as we finally pulled up close to Shakespeare Cliff and I was literally thrown into the water—not to start for the French coast, but to head for shore. According to CSA rules I had to start from the high-water mark, so when my hands starting scraping the pebbly beach I turned myself around and literally bummed my way backwards until the wet pebbles gave way to dry ones.

Then, almost three years since the idea of swimming the Channel first entered my head, the starter's horn sounded and I was on my way from

England to France, the hard way. But first I had to get back into the water, so there was more bum work to do. No doubt there have been more graceful water entries in Channel swimming history, but I can't imagine anyone was more pleased than me to undertake the challenge.

Once I started swimming I found it difficult to find my rhythm, and immediately I understood in my bones that the Channel was a different beast to the Lakes, the Shoalhaven River, or even the waters off Bondi Beach in Sydney, where I'd clocked up a lot of kilometres to get me comfortable with ocean swimming. I was also having a problem with my goggles—it turned out we'd got wool fat on them and they weren't doing the job, so I switched pairs a few hours into the swim.

About 5 hours from Dover, I was travelling well and pushing confidently through the grey, grainy water. My stroke was strong, the weather appeared to be holding firm, and, if anything, I felt better than I had over the first few hours. On the boat the mood was relaxed. Every time I turned my head to the right for a breath I could see someone looking down at me and clapping or giving me the thumbs up.

This was despite their mild annoyance. I discovered later that Marion was driving everyone barmy by loudly playing music by Australian rock legends Cold Chisel—over and over. She hoped the music would keep me psyched. What no-one, least of all Marion, knew was that due to my ear plugs and swimming cap, I couldn't hear much more than my own beating heart, so they were suffering in vain. That amused me no end when I found out.

Imperceptibly at first, the wind began to pick up. It continued to do so and it was soon obvious it was blowing in the opposite direction to the tide. This created swell and chop and began to make my life difficult.

With every stroke from then on the weather worsened, and while I felt no change in the water temperature, I could definitely feel myself being buffeted around. The extra swell forced my injured shoulder to work harder, so Reg did his best to protect me, angling his boat to take the initial brunt of the waves. When the wind and chop continued to pick up even that tactic was of little help. Nothing I'd done in the Pacific Ocean had prepared me for this.

AT SHAKESPEARE CLIFF, BUMMING MY WAY UP THE BEACH TO THE HIGH-WATER MARK
SO I COULD OFFICIALLY START MY CHANNEL CROSSING ATTEMPT ON 17 AUGUST 1998

Some 6 hours into the swim, the wind was blowing at what they call Force 8. Force 12 is a hurricane, so that gives you some indication of the nasty turn in the conditions. By now I was not just rising and falling, I was getting hammered by waves as if I were inside a washing machine. Riding the swell like a cork, I'd sink into a trough only to find the next wave barrelling over me. I'd cast a look over to the boat at such times and could see right over the deck, so violently was it listing in the swell. David Knight says he found the conditions frightening, and CSA observer Norm Trusty made the observation that the conditions were as bad as he'd ever seen for a solo swim. As he said at the time, 'If it was my swimmer in there, I'd have him out.'

I wasn't the only one in difficulty. At one point the surging sea nearly took down a helicopter that was carrying a cameraman hoping to get a dramatic aerial view of my swim. With the helicopter swooping low, a cresting wave took the pilot by surprise as it rushed up and over the skid, the helicopter's landing struts. Only the skill of the pilot stopped it being dragged into the Channel.

I can't say that I was surprised when David Harvey, who was wrapped in his spray jacket and holding onto the boat's rail as if it were a life buoy, relayed the message that Reg wanted me out of the water. His thoughts, backed up by his radar equipment in the cockpit, were that the weather wasn't going to improve. That being the case, there was no way I could complete my crossing.

This was not the news I—or David Harvey—wanted to hear. I was his protégé and although it affected him to see me struggling in the enormous swell, he wasn't ready to pull the plug on my dream. Joining me in a state of denial, he yelled, 'Go, you good thing!' and I swam on. I'd done so much work to get there, and I'd received so much help and love from so many people, that the idea of stopping seemed crazy. How could I disappoint so many, let alone myself?

I don't know if I had a delusion that I was Aquaman and could overcome the elements, but I refused to get out of the water and instead concentrated on each laboured stroke as wave after wave bashed me about. As each one hit me, I'd be tossed about as if I'd been dumped by a wave at the beach. Disorientated, I'd begin dog-paddling to get my bearings, then I'd start freestyling until the next wave knocked me over again.

I kept this up for another 2 hours and, due to the angle I was now swimming, I could make out the cliffs of France. Somewhat comically (in retrospect), I told myself to swim harder, that France was within reach—as if I'd been taking it easy up to this point. Around the same time, David Knight was in the water with me and he told me things were not looking good. I was reminded yet again of the weather report, but I was so close. I wasn't getting out now.

The mood on the boat was a pall of gloom, reflected on the faces of my supporters. Apart from the worsening weather, they knew my shoulder was aching as I continued to be pounded by the waves. I was now afforded almost no protection by the boat since, at such a slow speed, it couldn't reliably stay close to me without the risk of running me down in the rough seas. Even so, the sea would sometimes shunt the boat dangerously in my direction. At such times I lifted my head for a breath only to see, uncomfortably close to me, the exposed blades of the whirring propeller. On my next breath the boat had been hauled back and it seemed a mile away.

Wally and David had been stoically fulfilling their duties as support swimmers but I went within myself at this point. As in Hawaii, I forced myself to repeat affirmations. I had to convince myself that I could do this and it would all be over before I knew it. I also told myself that things could be much worse. I remembered talking to Susie Maroney a few times in the lead-up and she told me about her swim from Florida to Cuba, a monster effort that took her 48 hours. Two days! How could I think to complain about this when compared to that?

Nine hours into the swim, Reg came to the boat's rail to tell me that for the past 3 hours I had actually been losing ground. I'd gone backwards. That broke me. Any resolve I had that I could somehow push through disappeared like a puff of smoke. Why am I doing this?, I thought. Get me out of here.

I was about 10 kilometres from Calais when I conceded defeat. The elements had beaten me, as they'd beaten many better than me. I was hauled onto the boat, sore and sorry, and could only drop my head and curse my luck as the boat turned about and headed back to England.

On board now, in a tracksuit and wrapped up in towels, I had an even better perspective of the conditions and I found it hard to believe I'd actually been out there. We were rocking so much that not only was one of the film crew guys as sick as a dog but so was Reg, a fisherman as seasoned as they come. I was amazed at how long it took us to get back and I considered how insignificant we all were in this sea: how helpless we are, for all our human achievements, in the face of Mother Nature.

In the cabin, the mood wasn't good. I felt awful, as if I'd somehow let everyone down. I felt particularly bad for David Knight, since he'd helped convince Gatorade to fund the documentary to the tune of $100,000 and now it looked like being a dud. Who wants to watch a documentary about a bloke *not* swimming the English Channel?

Sensing my despondency and guilt, the sound man told me not to worry and assured me it would still be a great doco. 'It'll be real,' he said, 'and in real life dreams don't always come true.'

As waterlogged as I was, that permeated right through. What do you mean?, I said to myself. When you work hard enough dreams must come true. I'd seen it for myself in Hawaii.

DESPITE MY EXHAUSTION IT WASN'T EASY TO SLEEP that night. My equilibrium was out of whack from the swim and the long, sombre journey back to Folkestone, which took 3 hours under full steam. I could still feel the violent rhythm of the ocean and my shoulder ached, even after the most satisfying hot bath in recorded history. The thought of returning to Australia with my tail between my legs played over and over in my head like a bad movie. I decided we had to give this another go.

I still felt the same when morning came, and I told David Harvey that I was willing to give it another crack. He said he'd been thinking the same thing. But it wasn't just up to us, and I was incredibly anxious as we approached Reg to see if there was another opportunity in the coming days or weeks to give it another try. There was no guarantee I'd get another chance.

The best we could get from Reg was, 'Let's wait and see.'

The others couldn't keep their lives on hold indefinitely on that basis. So, while David Harvey and I stayed on in England, my brother Don returned to Canada, David Knight went home to take a scheduled holiday with his family in Australia, Wally and his wife, Natalie, went to visit relatives in Croatia, and the documentary crew returned to Australia, the cost of keeping them waiting in England being prohibitive.

Essentially, I spent the first week asleep. That was an indication of how much the swim had taken out of me, despite my being so well prepared. The next week I got intensive physio on my shoulder, which was still sore and tight (coincidentally, the physio treatment was provided by the last person to swim from Calais to Dover before the CSA stopped recognising the feat, because, comparatively, it was considered the easier option). And I discussed with David shortening my stroke length to reduce strain on it should we get another chance.

Then a call came through from Reg. He had a day free—30 August—and the weather reports were promising. Delighted at the news, we hit the phones to inform the crew.

Showing their level of support and the closeness of the team, everyone but Marion and George was able to return. Wally and Natalie had spent only 4 hours in the company of long-lost relatives before they had to turn the car around and come straight back. Don returned from Canada (without Megan and Sean), while the documentary crew made another gruelling 24-hour flight across the world to get to Dover in time.

David Knight, meantime, was skiing with his family at Thredbo in Australia's Snowy Mountains, about 8 hours' drive south of Sydney. I filled him in on my second chance and asked him to wish me luck. 'Wish you luck? What are you talking about? I'm on my way.'

I would *never* have expected David to drop a family holiday to cross the world to be with me. He'd already proved his feelings and loyalty

AT DEAL, KENT, IN 1998 WITH MY CHANNEL-CROSSING SUPPORT CREW. CLOCKWISE FROM LEFT: DAVID HARVEY, DAVID KNIGHT, GEORGE LAWLER, WALLY BRUMNIACH, ME, LISA SAAD, MARION, DON'S DAUGHTER MEGAN AND NATALIE BRUMNIACH

to me by training with me and swimming with me on my first Channel effort. But time wasn't in David's favour and, even though he was a support swimmer, I couldn't wait for him to arrive.

IN AN ATTEMPT TO MAKE THE MOST OF THE CONDITIONS, Reg decided the swim should begin at 5am. So it was pitch dark when we again boarded *The Viking Princess* at Folkestone and chugged around the coast to Shakespeare Cliff. Beneath us, the water was black and impenetrable, and I think if I hadn't been so pumped to be in the water on the way to France, getting in would have been an unsettling prospect.

In keeping with the CSA rules, I had to repeat my less-than-elegant 'bumming' effort up to the high-water mark, then it was back in the water, greased up like a truck axle, where I pushed through the slight swell and began to fall into a smooth, steady stroke pattern.

Into the first hour I was stroking well and feeling comfortable, despite the darkness. The lights of the Dover coast were still close enough to make out, and I tried not to think about that for it was a none too subtle reminder of how far I had to go. Nevertheless, I continued at a good pace and David, watching over me from the boat, seemed pleased with my progress.

David Harvey spent his time coordinating my breaks, watching my style and counting my stroke rate, which he had determined was optimal at 60 strokes per minute. I was so familiar with my stroke rate that when David told me to speed up or slow down I'd never be more than a few strokes a minute outside the target.

After 2 hours on my own, Wally was able to join me and I appreciated the company. While you're swimming you're not chatting, but just to see someone I knew swimming along beside me—as he'd done most memorably in the Shoalhaven River—gave me a lift and I felt strongest at such times.

Despite this, my shoulder continued to give me trouble and I tried not to think about what would happen if it got considerably worse. To have to pull out again would have broken my heart. To help with the pain, anti-inflammatories were put in my drink containers which, every half hour, David Harvey would cast out to me on a fishing-rod-like device, hauling them back in when I'd had my fill.

Depending on the swell, there were times when I was able to see right into the boat's main cabin. One time I spied Don sipping tea, eating cake and watching Formula One motor racing on the small television Reg had installed. How I would have loved to be up there with him. Hope you're comfortable, mate, I said wryly to myself. Let me know if there's anything else I can get you.

David Knight, meantime, was making an incredible journey to be by my side. After our phone call he and his family hastily packed their belongings and drove from the snowfields back to Sydney's eastern suburbs. After quickly repacking, he made his way to the airport and booked the next flight to London. The first available flight went via Bangkok so he took it, calling me when he got there some 9 hours later. (By this time I was less than a day away from the wake-up call that would signal Channel Day Mark II).

After a delay in Bangkok, David then got his connecting flight to Heathrow, a 15-hour journey that can exhaust the most seasoned traveller. David was indeed exhausted when he arrived in London, but there was no time to waste, so he hired a car and drove non-stop to Dover, arriving around 7am, about 2 hours after I'd begun my swim.

Anyone else would have given up at that point, satisfied they'd at least given it their best shot, but David wasn't done. After being told that a helicopter wasn't allowed to return to shore with one passenger fewer than when it departed, he began scouting around the docks at Dover trying to find a boat to take him out into the Channel and, he hoped, catch *The Viking Princess*. At that time of day most boats had already left to trawl the waters, but David was fortunate enough to find two men about to go fishing and he explained the rather unusual situation to them and asked if they could help him. They initially said no, but David persuaded them with £100. Then they told him they only had two tanks of petrol, one to take them out and one to bring them back in. When that first tank ran dry they would have to turn back, no matter what.

The fishermen had a Global Positioning Satellite system on board but it was new and neither of them knew how to work it. This meant they had to find us by liaising with *The Viking Princess* via mobile phones and a two-way radio, though I was, of course, unaware of any of this at the time. If that wasn't problematic enough (there are not exactly a lot of 'landmarks' at sea by which to guide someone), there were still a few more obstacles for David to overcome, as the first tank of fuel was fast running out.

'We've got to turn back,' one of the men announced, but David somehow convinced him to keep going a little longer. This despite the fact that many of the vessels plying the Channel are enormous supertankers which can take kilometres to come to a stop. It is therefore unwise to be bobbing around out there without petrol.

ALL ABOARD *THE VIKING PRINCESS* MOTORING FROM FOLKESTONE TO SHAKESPEARE CLIFF FOR THE START OF MY FIRST CHANNEL ATTEMPT ON 17 AUGUST 1998

Eventually, after some desperate communications work ('You see that ferry? We're near that'), they spotted *The Viking Princess*. After a non-stop journey that had begun 50 hours earlier in Australia, David finally rejoined my Channel team. Without a moment's pause, he slipped into his wetsuit and goggles and leapt into the water beside me.

'Hello, mate,' he said.

Talk about surprised.

When we pulled away from the dock at Folkestone to go to Shakespeare Cliff I had assumed David hadn't made it. When he plunged into the water beside me I just couldn't believe it. His commitment to do what he did was extraordinary. He'd left his family in the middle of a holiday and crossed the world on a mercy dash. All to be with his mate, and to follow through on his promise to help me achieve my goal. How incredible is that?

By this stage I'd been swimming for 6 hours and I was really starting to hurt. Pain was beginning to slip through my defences and denials and I was feeling every stroke. But when David appeared like an apparition my spirits lifted, though I didn't have the energy, or the time, to convey anything to him other than a broad smile. It was similar to the inspiration I got from Johnno's words in Hawaii in 1995. How could I possibly not get through this when so many people had given up so much to help me?

So on I swam, with David at my side. No words were spoken after the initial greeting, nor did they need to be. Everything that needed to be communicated could be felt. I was rejuvenated and my body found a hidden reserve of endorphins which made me feel almost euphoric, even when David was back on board and I was alone again in the water.

Mother Nature was a lot kinder to me the second time around, and I owe her one. The seas didn't rise up against me and the wind didn't come to push me backwards. Instead, the swell remained manageable and from the ninth hour onwards I could see France and believe that I was going to get there.

Almost 12 hours into the swim we reached a critical point and ahead of me, beckoning me, was the Cap Gris-Nez lighthouse south-west of Calais. The tide was about to change and, as David Harvey yelled out to me from the boat, if I didn't beat it, I would have no chance of finishing the swim.

This worried the hell out of me and, though exhausted, I tried as hard as I could to lift my stroke rate. The thought of getting so close and again being unable to make it horrified me, and as I pushed on, I reaffirmed just why I was putting myself through this.

I emptied my tank in the next hour, using every reserve of energy and resolve to beat the tide and swim until my hands brushed French soil. As if it was a Hollywood movie, I beat the changing tide and ran aground on the sandy beach at Wissant just as the day's dreary cover of cloud parted and the sun broke through. I felt elated. David Knight was next to me in the water by this stage and we hugged each other. We'd done it. The documentary crew had what they wanted, everyone else was overjoyed, particularly David Knight, David Harvey and Wally, who were by now on the beach and treating me to a standing ovation. I could feel their euphoria lift me one last time as I backed up to the high-water line to officially complete the crossing.

When my bum hit dry sand, the official clock stopped at 12 hours and 55 minutes. I lay back, looked into the sky and felt flooded with relief. Deciding to select a memento for myself, I picked out a gnarled stone and slipped it into my swimmers because there was nowhere else to put it. There it stayed as the film crew rushed over to me and asked me the inevitable: 'How do you feel?'

'Sometimes you win and sometimes you lose, but I hope today I've won for all the little boys and girls around the world in wheelchairs. If they need someone to look up to, hopefully they've got someone to look up to now.'

LITTLE DID I KNOW AT THE TIME that the chapter wasn't quite closed on the English Channel. While we were all still in the flush of excitement at having completed the crossing, David Knight announced he wanted to give it a go. He first considered the idea during my crossing when Reg had suggested to him that, with all he was putting in as a support swimmer, he could do it himself. David's reply to Reg was that he'd do it when he was 40. I'm sure he hoped everyone would forget by then.

Not me. At his 39th birthday in Westport, Connecticut (where David was then living with his family), I said to him, 'Only 12 months to get your Channel swim in.'

'Thanks for reminding me,' he replied, without sarcasm.

It was enough to drive him on. And then some. Not only did David plan to cross the Channel but he wanted to complete a double crossing, which means that when you touch France you turn around and swim back to England. I'd wanted to do the same but when I finally reached Calais there was no way I could have attempted to swim back to England, having lost so much during the aborted attempt.

David had already followed up on his goal to complete the Hawaiian Ironman in 1999 and I could see no reason why the Channel would be beyond him. While he didn't have my luxury of being a professional athlete, and instead would have to go to work every day as usual, he has a determination and life force like few people I know.

So it meant the world to me in 2004 to be able to do for David what he did for me. To give something back to him, to be part of his support crew—which included his mates Liam and Pierre—gave me more pleasure, I can honestly say, than swimming the Channel myself. I absolutely loved the experience, clapping and cheering him on from the boat and, when the time came, jumping in with him to keep him company in the water.

I remember 8 hours into the swim he asked me to call his wife, Andrea, and tell her he loved her and it was a duty I fulfilled with a lump in my throat. I felt honoured to be included in his life in such a way. I would not have wanted to be anywhere else in the world.

As with my second swim, David couldn't fault the weather and he completed his crossing in 13 hours and 4 minutes, just 9 minutes more than it took me, uncannily close I think. While Liam secured a memento on David's behalf, David took a break at the water's edge (10 minutes was the maximum allowed) to eat some food.

In retrospect this was a mistake. Eating takes heat away from the body and David should have got straight back in the water, especially as the outside temperature was colder than the water. So David was cold by the time he resumed swimming and I don't think he ever regained enough heat, which made his return attempt considerably more trying.

The hours went by and David pushed slowly on, crawling his way back to England. By the time he'd been in the water a total of 19 hours I could sense he was really struggling. He was also getting disorientated and constantly drifting away from the boat. Then it was my time to join him in the water again. 'Can you please get closer to the boat?' I asked him repeatedly, but he looked at me like I was a ghost and took no notice, continuing to swim off course. It got to the point where I had to endure his strokes on my back as, like a tug boat, I tried to angle him closer to the pilot boat.

Finally, he seemed to get the message that he had to change course and I could momentarily relax. But we were barely moving now and it hurt me to see him in such pain. I knew by then he wasn't going to make it but I kept that to myself, for I wanted to be positive for him. He'd asked me many times to keep him in the water.

When Reg appeared at the boat's rail after David had been going for 20 hours I asked him for an update. 'We're going at about 1 mile an hour,' Reg said. 'At this rate, and under these conditions, it could take another 15 hours to get back. That's providing the conditions stay okay.'

Hearing that, David knew he couldn't make it and he finally relented. 'That's enough,' he said. 'Let's get back to England and eat some eggs.'

Drawn, pale and suffering hypothermia, David was helped into the boat.

Sitting in the cabin with him I was choked up with emotion and pride. When I first met David he was unfit and overweight; now, here he was, a veteran of the Hawaiian Ironman, and a successful Channel swimmer. It was a phenomenal achievement and I told him so. 'Don't be dejected, you've just joined an elite club. How many people do you think have swum the English Channel and completed a Hawaiian Ironman?'

Slowly the colour came back into his face and David's life force began to return. 'The Great Man,' as I call him, started to come back and, incredibly, he was soon entertaining the crew as if he hadn't just slogged for nearly a full day across one of the world's most tempestuous waterways. I could only sit back and admire him.

IN AUGUST 2004, SIX YEARS AFTER DAVID KNIGHT (LEFT) SO MEMORABLY SUPPORTED ME, I JOINED PIERRE (RIGHT) TO HELP DAVID IN HIS SUCCESSFUL CHANNEL BID

It was sitting there with David that brought my Channel experience full circle. Looking at him, I knew I would drop everything at any time to be with him if he needed me. As I would for Johnno. He believed in my dream, he helped get the documentary made and sold, and he put himself on the line for me, physically, financially and emotionally.

If the Channel was partly about showing young children in wheelchairs that their future was limitless, it was also about mateship and bonding and how these have the power to transform our lives.

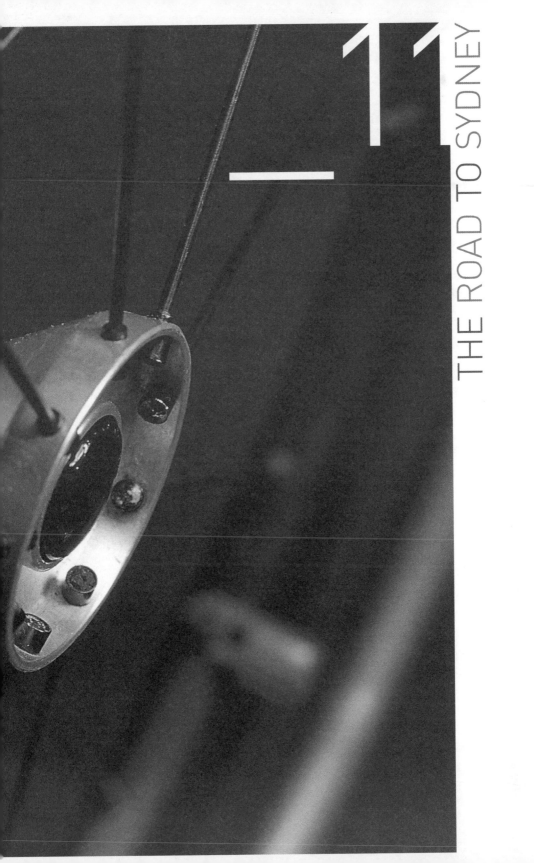

11 THE ROAD TO SYDNEY

A FEW WEEKS AFTER RETURNING HOME FROM ENGLAND, the launch of my Channel-swim documentary *Against Wind and Tide* was held in Sydney. Out from Florida to help me celebrate the red-carpet affair was Cynthia, who'd been in England to support me for the swim.

Cynthia, I think, had a view of us getting engaged at some stage and her coming to Sydney, and subsequently living with me in Penrith, was a kind of trial run. Yet again I was living for the moment and, while I enjoyed Cynthia's company enormously, I wasn't thinking about a long-term relationship. For one thing, I didn't feel there was the space in my life. My sport was taking up more and more time and, with the Paralympics as a goal, that was going to continue to be the case for a good while yet.

I'm almost embarrassed to say it, but once again, after a few weeks, I began to think the relationship with Cynthia wasn't working out. Though it wasn't something I'd contemplated at all when I stayed with her in Florida, I began to think we were poorly matched. By this stage, any superficial

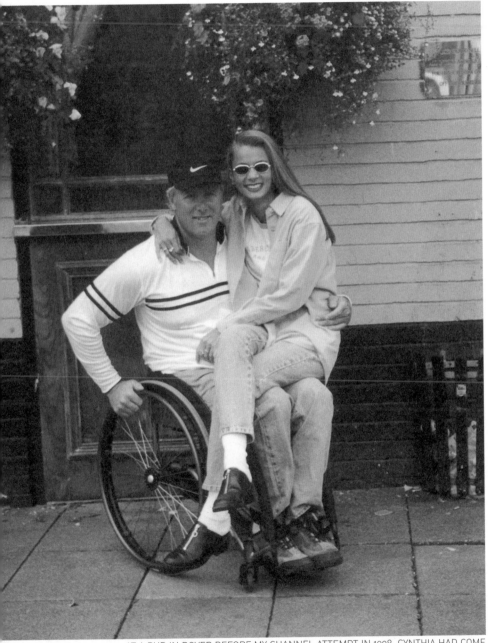

AT A PUB IN DOVER BEFORE MY CHANNEL ATTEMPT IN 1998. CYNTHIA HAD COME
ALL THE WAY FROM FLORIDA TO SUPPORT ME

differences between us—the things we ate, the television programs we watched, the time we took to get dressed and out of the house, *anything*—I whipped up relentlessly inside my head, until it seemed obvious to me that the relationship wasn't going to work out and I ended it. Cynthia was back in Florida by Christmas. Of course, all this says much more about me, and where I was at that stage in my life, than it does about Cynthia.

Alone again at Penrith, I set myself the task of losing the extra weight I was carrying. While it had helped me to cope with prolonged exposure to the cold currents, I felt very uncomfortable carrying the additional bulk around and I wasn't lingering too long in front of any mirrors.

Losing weight was not purely for cosmetic reasons. Typically, even before setting off for the Channel, I'd spent a lot of time thinking about a future goal, something I'd like to take on when I returned to Australia. This was made easier than it might otherwise have been because Sydney, my home town, was to host both the 2000 Olympic and Paralympic Games.

It was a sign of how comfortable I now felt with myself that I would even consider entering wheelchair-only races in a sporting tournament designed purely for people who are physically challenged. Ironically, the less I felt defined and restricted by my paraplegia (after Hawaii and the Channel I saw myself as John Maclean the athlete, not John Maclean the paraplegic athlete), the more comfortable I felt competing in sporting events designed for athletes in wheelchairs. I'd come a long way from the 22-year-old accident victim who, so desperate to believe he would walk again, would torture himself by struggling about on crutches instead of using a wheelchair.

Having said that, I have to admit that in addition to the Paralympic Games, I knew there would be a 1500-metre wheelchair race, a demonstration event, at the Olympic Games. The odds of my making the worldwide field of eight were incredibly slim. Still, I couldn't help but think how amazing it would be to be part of the Olympics, on the biggest stage there is.

Wheelchair racing in its purest form was something I'd never done and I knew there were many outstanding athletes in the field, both in Australia and elsewhere. While I'd done marathon distances in my racing wheelchair in triathlon (which was more about survival and making the finish line), shorter-distance track racing was something else entirely, and there was the very real chance that I was setting myself up for a fall.

What did I have to prove anymore, anyway?

Nothing, I guess, at least in terms of proving something to myself. But I think that by this stage I was simply competing and setting myself goals because that's what I'd always loved doing since I was a boy. I thrived on the challenges inherent in athletic competition. I never would have predicted my attitude to this a decade earlier, but wheelchair racing was simply a new athletic field, one as tough and complex as anything else I could have attempted.

First, though, that weight had to go.

Under the guidance of dietitian Helen O'Connor, I began losing it. Obviously the mammoth meals I had been eating to bulk up for the Channel were off the menu, particularly the carbohydrate-rich foods that had given me the fuel for my crossing.

In stark contrast to what I'd had pre-Channel, nothing passed my lips the first two days aside from freshly squeezed orange juice and water. During the next two days fruit was added to the list of acceptable foods. Then on days five, six and seven, vegetables were included. Even after only a week, I could see my body changing and, while I'm sure it's different for everyone, I felt fantastic and more alert than I had in a long while.

After the asceticism of that first week I just ate sensibly and cut out carbohydrates. Even though I wasn't doing much exercise—beyond some gentle swimming and pushing myself around in my chair—I dropped most of the 20 kilograms I'd put on in six weeks.

Once back to my optimum weight I set myself the challenge of competing in a 10-kilometre wheelchair race around the historic Rocks district of Sydney on Australia Day, 26 January 1999. After getting back from the Channel I'd met with Jenni Banks, a wheelchair racing coach. I told her my aspiration was to be a Paralympian; she said she thought she could help me, and together we formulated an accelerated plan to put me in a position to make the Australian Paralympic team despite my inexperience.

The challenge, Jenni said, was considerable. Wheelchair racing, unlike the marathons I'd been doing, needed specific skills that would take a good deal of time to learn. Only using my racing chair on open roads, I'd never had to learn too much about chair handling during close-in racing, nor did I have to be particularly tactically minded. On the other hand, my aerobic capacity was well established and Jenni saw in me someone who was willing to put in the work and training that would be needed. That's often half the battle.

The plan Jenni and I devised would see me race all over the world in the 18 months leading up to the Games, trying to equal, or better, the qualifying times that I needed to make the Paralympics. These would not be easily acquired as, generally, they match the time achieved by the silver medallist in the previous Paralympic Games. Jenni and I figured I'd be best placed trying to achieve as many qualifying times as possible—that is, trying to qualify in every distance I could, from 1500 metres to the marathon—to give myself the greatest opportunity of making the Australian team.

My road to Sydney began at the Rocks in the Oz Day 10K, as it is known. As far as Jenni and I were concerned, this was simply a race in which I'd test the waters. It was a gorgeous place to make my debut. As anyone who's toured Sydney will know, the Rocks borders Sydney Harbour, surely one of the world's most beautiful waterways. The race winds through the various streets around the harbour and, had I not been hell bent on finishing as high up as possible, it would have been a dream route to linger over.

Out of a high-class international field of 50 (both men and women), I finished tenth, in spectacular style. So distracted was I with holding off a Canadian competitor beside me, that I crashed at speed into the finishing barricade. Powering home, my head was down and my bum was up, so to speak, and I simply lifted my head to check my bearings a little too late. The impact sent my chair slamming onto its side, snapping it clean through. For my troubles I was bruised and grazed. Jenni and Johnno, who were there watching, raced over to ensure I was okay.

Some might suggest it was an attention-seeking manoeuvre, for the following day's papers covered my accident and race participation at some expense to the other competitors, but I can assure you it wasn't. It was the result of an overflow of competitive juices. And I was delighted, notwithstanding my slight injuries. It showed me that I was at least prepared to give this thing a red-hot go. As did my time: a full minute faster than Jenni had optimistically predicted.

I HAVE PREVIOUSLY MENTIONED THE ADVANTAGES and disadvantages of my distinct type of paraplegia. In a day-to-day context, being incomplete means I can stand on my left leg supported by crutches for very brief periods and, as a consequence, I have better mobility than a paraplegic who has no feeling in their legs at all. I am extremely thankful for this. In racing terms, however, being incomplete often puts me at a slight disadvantage. Wheelchair racing comes down to power-to-weight ratios, which basically means that the lighter you are the stronger you (potentially) are. Double amputees or complete paraplegics—those who have no feeling in their legs and thus no muscle bulk—carry all their weight and power in their upper body. In purely racing terms, they are better off than I am if we are fairly evenly matched above the waist. But my most significant disadvantage was my inexperience at short-distance racing. To combat that I vowed to open myself up to learning, and, continuing a trend I'd started with the Channel, to put aside my ego and not be afraid to ask for help and advice.

In every field there is someone better equipped and more experienced than you are, so why not gain the benefit of their knowledge? I had so much to learn about racing tactics, racing posture, wheelchair types and equipment modification. There was no chance I could stumble upon all the answers myself in time to qualify for the Paralympics. I didn't see the wisdom in going it alone.

Early in 1999 I secured a training partner in Paul Nunnari, who became a paraplegic after being hit by a car when he was just 11 years old. It helped enormously to have someone to work with, particularly someone as gracious and giving as Paul, who had a few years' racing under his belt. I also started to speak to people like Saul Mendoza, from Mexico; Heinz

Frei, from Switzerland; and Jeff Adams, from Canada, three of the most accomplished wheelchair athletes in the world. Frei, for instance, is one of the fittest men I have ever met and, to my mind, he just doesn't get fatigued. Paralysed from about his chest down he is phenomenally strong, as his marathon world record of 1 hour and 20 minutes attests.

I had much to learn from people like Frei, Mendoza and Adams, and perhaps it was because none of them saw me as a threat that they so readily helped out. I bombarded them with detailed questions. What glove type would be best? What wheelchair height would maximise my thrust? What rim size would best suit me? What make and model of wheelchair should I use, for that matter? And so on. I knew that no matter how much training I did I was not in Frei and Mendoza's league. But I was determined to give myself the best opportunity I could, and I was willing to work.

It also didn't hurt that, as a child and young adult, I was more of a sprinter than a distance athlete. My Ironman races had forced me to confront 40-kilometre-plus distances on my racing chair, but my muscle make-up had always been more attuned to sprinting, and this stood me in good stead as the months rolled by.

In broad terms I progressed quickly and I know this infuriated a small number of my compatriots in the sport of wheelchair racing, some of whom did not accept me at all. This put me in an uncomfortable position and it hurt me, for I never considered myself a threat to anyone, nor did I ever intend to put anyone's nose out of joint by striving to become a Paralympian. As far as I was concerned, I'd set myself a goal of representing my country at the Paralympic Games—a huge honour in anyone's eyes—and I was doing all I could to achieve that.

But, as was illustrated starkly by a particular episode that was just around the corner, some in the wheelchair racing fraternity didn't see things that way, and, generally speaking (for there were, of course, many exceptional people in the sport who gave me plenty of encouragement), I wasn't really embraced or made to feel particularly welcome. So when I went away as part of the Australian Paralympic athletics train-on squad, I missed the personal connections I'd had with my training teams in the past.

It's probably unfair to make this comparison, since my teams for Hawaii and the Channel were made up of friends and family, but nevertheless I never felt I fitted in. In any case, I stuck with it and Paul Nunnari was a big help and a source of strength as I travelled the world. I may not have felt embraced, but I consistently performed well as I ate, slept and trained with the Paralympics in mind.

IT WAS ABOUT THIS TIME THAT I CONNECTED with another couple of people who would play important roles in my life. The first was American Marc Robinson, who was living in Australia with his wife, Lori, and their sons, Jason and Brian. Marc was president of the Australian arm of an American consumer health care company. I'd been invited to give a talk to the company's senior managers at a Sydney harbourside restaurant, and it was here I met Marc when he approached me after my presentation and told me how affected he had been by what I had to say. A few days later Marc called me and asked me if I would speak to the company's factory workers. Following that talk, Marc invited me to his home for a barbecue with his family.

From that point on, Marc and I became friends, and it was a friendship that endured when he returned home to the States to take up a position as president of the drug company Pfizer's consumer health care division. I've been lucky enough to visit Marc and his family a few times at their New Jersey home, and each time I return home with a new respect for him. It's difficult to say eloquently enough what it is about Marc that appeals to me, but I suppose what I admire and respect about him most is his lack of guile and his absolute dedication to his family. Marc is a completely genuine guy who, admirably, considering his high-powered position, has struck a balance between work and family. He is no corporate slave who only really sees his family on weekends. Whenever there is a conflict between work and family, Marc will always put his family first. And I see in him a model for the kind of man I hope to be when I one day have a family of my own.

As I was getting to know Marc, I began seeing a woman with whom I'd gone to high school. I'd reconnected with Malena at a school reunion which, ironically, neither of us was all that keen on attending. Malena had been one of the school stunners. Nothing had changed and we gravitated into each other's orbits and caught up on each other's lives. Obviously there were a lot of questions for me, being in a wheelchair, but I did my best to steer any conversation away from me, which is how I like it.

Malena lived in Sydney's eastern suburbs and I started to spend a lot of time there. It was a different world to the less pretentious western suburbs where I grew up and lived, and while I felt a little self-conscious at first, I got to enjoy the slightly glitzier culture: the cafes, bars and swish restaurants.

I had a great time with Malena although, typically, my thoughts rarely extended beyond the immediate. I'd never consciously decided to have a relationship with her. It was something that just happened, and after about six months together, as I'd done with Cynthia, I began to find things I didn't like as I subconsciously thought about moving on before things got too serious. So I convinced myself that, among other things, Malena did not fit my physical ideal—and I told her so. As you'd expect, she didn't take that well at all, saying that if I didn't like her the way she was I could go to hell. Understandably, her language was a little richer than that, but you get the picture.

In retrospect, I deliberately sabotaged the relationship although, at the time, I told myself—and believed it—that things just weren't working out. But in no way had I made a genuine effort to give myself to the relationship. I was happy to float along, have a good time and get out before I got in too deep. It was by now a well-established pattern.

Oddly enough, while my callous remarks ended the relationship, Malena and I remained friends, which says a lot about her capacity for forgiveness and understanding.

WHILE I WAS BUILDING AND STUFFING UP RELATIONSHIPS, at the same time I was also continuing my Paralympics push. In April 2000 I competed in the famous Boston marathon and finished fourth in the wheelchair category, and it was shortly after that I knew for certain that I'd qualified for the Games. In all, I achieved qualifying standards in the 1500 metres, 5000 metres, 10,000 metres, the marathon and the 4 x 400 metres relay. Previously, merely qualifying would have been the culmination of my goal, but I now began to think about winning medals.

It was around this time that Chris Nunn, the head coach of the Australian Paralympic athletics team, called to inform me that Australia, being the host nation, had been given a wild-card slot for the 1500-metre demonstration race at the Olympic Games. Was I interested?, he asked.

Was I ever! Here was an opportunity to represent my country at the Olympic Games, the pinnacle of world sport.

Chris told me that there were two other guys interested in representing our country, one being Paul Nunnari, the other Kurt Fearnley, a young up-and-comer and a powerful, graceful racer (who would go on to win numerous Paralympic medals in 2000 and 2004, including gold in the 5000 metres and the marathon at the Athens Paralympic Games). I replied that, no matter what method he used to choose among the three of us, I wanted to be given a chance. By the end of the conversation, however, Chris seemed to have changed his mind. Perhaps it was because he didn't want to have to choose who'd take the spot, but he suddenly decided none of us would get the wild card. We'd have to earn entry on our own merits by racing the best in the world at a European meet later in the year.

In the meantime, I continued with my training and competition schedule, which included a meet in Gothenburg, Sweden, early in 2000. Every now and then in an athlete's life, he or she has one of those meets when everything goes right. Gothenburg was one. I nailed it, winning the 800 metres, the 5000 metres, the 10,000 metres and coming second to Jeff Adams in the 1500 metres. The field wasn't quite the best of the best, but there were some very accomplished wheelchair athletes in the various races and it did my confidence a world of good. The Boston marathon fourth placing was great, but this made me feel like I belonged, that I wasn't an impostor. No matter what my detractors said or felt, I knew I was one of the best wheelchair racers in the world.

AUSTRALIAN TEAMMATE AND CLOSE FRIEND PAUL NUNNARI (LEFT) SITS BEHIND ME IN A 5000-METRE RACE
IN SWITZERLAND ABOUT A YEAR OUT FROM THE SYDNEY PARALYMPIC GAMES IN 2000

By this stage I'd been informed of the selection criteria for the 1500-metre wheelchair race at the Olympic Games. It had been decided that the starting field would be selected from four heats and semifinals to be held at a meet in Delemont, Switzerland.

Lining up for my heat I saw a steely-faced Heinz Frei, who, though 40, was every bit as good as he'd always been. I felt that if I could stick with him, he could carry me through to the semifinals and, hopefully, beyond. But Heinz is typically a slow starter, so I knew when the gun went, I would have to take it out fast then wait for Heinz to inevitably catch me. When that happened, I hoped I'd have enough left to ride his wake to the finish line.

Heinz is the nicest guy you could meet and he has always been gracious to me. He even helped me get a special glove made similar to one he'd developed and had been using for years. The peculiar—and distinctive—thing about Heinz's glove was that, due to a small piece of plastic, it made a clicking sound when he pushed his wheel rim. This meant that when our heat was underway, and I'd managed to stay in the lead with a lap to go, I could hear him coming before I could see him. Not that I could hold him off. As I'd expected, he came up on my shoulder and raced ahead. Fortunately, my plan was sound enough—I had enough energy left to slip in behind him and hold on to second place and qualify for the semifinals.

So far so good, though unfortunately, Paul Nunnari didn't make it through his heat. Kurt Fearnley did, however, leaving two Aussies in the final sixteen. Only half that number would make the final. The first three place-getters in each semifinal would qualify automatically for the final, then the two athletes with the next best times.

My semifinal contained a hot field and again I chose similar tactics to those that had got me through my heat. For the first three laps I was in the lead or thereabouts, but then, no matter how hard I pushed, I began to get reeled in by the experienced racers. Frenchman Joel Jeannot picked me up, then American Scott Hollenbeck. Yet, despite a near-collision with Jeannot, I held on and finished third.

I could hardly believe it. I was on my way to the Olympic Games. Well, for the moment, at least. The euphoria had barely sunk in when I heard there had been a protest and the race result was under review. Apparently, when Jeannot cut in front of me, the swerve I made to avoid him caused someone behind me to crash. I'd been only vaguely aware of the crash at the time and certainly didn't feel I was in any way responsible.

There was a chance I would be disqualified and I was extremely anxious awaiting the review, which was overseen by a video referee. When the result was announced I had mixed feelings. The judges deemed that Jeannot's swerve had created a domino effect behind him and it was Jeannot, not me, who was responsible for the crash. He was then disqualified. Despite that, the judges decided the race would be re-run.

Considering I felt I'd qualified fairly, this was a huge blow and I had to lift myself all over again. I told myself that if I had done it once I could do it again and I mentally prepared myself as best I could.

Leading in to the replayed semifinal, which took place a few hours later, I lay on gymnastic mats in a neighbouring gym and repeatedly reassured myself that I was good enough to be here and good enough to make the final. My meet in Sweden had proved that beyond question. I just wouldn't allow self-doubt to take hold. It's one of my strong points that I'm usually able to keep it in check. I told myself that I was one of the best 1500-metre racers in the world and I believed it. The proof was already there and now I just had to grit my teeth and prove it again.

By the time I was back up on the start line I really felt I could do it. Knowing I didn't have a sprinter's kick, I sped out of the blocks, so to speak, and led the field around the first bend. Then the second. Then the third. The rest of the field was playing cat and mouse and letting me go, hoping to pick me up in the final stages. Driving myself, I stayed in the lead until there were 200 metres left to go and I screamed at myself to keep it up as I heard the chasing pack get closer and closer. Someone passed me over my right shoulder, then, 20 metres on, I was passed again. With 100 metres to go, and flying along at around 32 kilometres per hour, I was holding grimly on to third place, striving to keep my form together as my muscles began to seize up.

But I could hear someone breathing down my neck and drawing closer and closer as the finish line approached. Under his attack, whoever he was, the finish line seemed so far away and I didn't know if I could keep him at bay. He was right beside me when we hit the line and I had no idea who'd got their nose in front. For five excruciatingly long minutes we waited for the photo-finish results. Then they came through.

I had finished third by just 1/100th of a second. I was going to the Olympic Games.

12 THE CRASH

THE MARGIN OF MY THIRD PLACING MAY HAVE BEEN SLIGHT, but it was inversely proportional to my delight (which I managed to keep a lid on until it was clear there would be no protest and that the race result would stand). I'd qualified for the Olympic Games. I would be representing Australia, in my home town, on the world's largest multi-sport stage. I recalled the joy I had all those years ago when, at age 12, I won the Australian 1500-metre walk title in Canberra. Like then, I was utterly convinced I'd reached some kind of sporting nirvana and I told myself as much: 'It doesn't get any better than this'.

At least, that's what I thought for all of 30 minutes, the time it took me to notice that other Australian wheelchair racers, who were participating in other events during the meet, weren't sharing my joy. Paul Nunnari was obviously and understandably disappointed, he'd missed out on a place of his own (as had Kurt Fearnley, ever so narrowly). But the vibe from many others in the squad was not congratulatory or supportive.

This is one of the highlights of my life, I thought, yet I feel so flat and lonely. There was no energy around me, no positivity, and I reflected on my sense of isolation from my loved ones, the group who had supported me through my most difficult battles. Here, with a few notable exceptions, I felt like an outsider and that was underlined by the apparent lack of interest in what I had done.

My impression was confirmed when, shortly after the race, I was confronted by a fellow squad member who told me, in no uncertain terms, that they didn't share my joy. Considering this came right after one of the great moments in my athletic career, it really knocked me about.

As I gathered from the diatribe, I was seen as an upstart who hadn't served his apprenticeship, yet was already taking away some of the spotlight from others who'd been wheelchair racing for years. Moreover, I came into the sport with sponsors already behind me, and if I continued to attract more sponsors (because of the profile I'd built up doing Hawaii and the Channel) it would be to the detriment of others (the logic being that sponsorship potential for wheelchair athletes was finite—a view I totally disagree with).

'It's okay for you,' I was told. 'You weren't born in this position. You had an accident and got money for your accident. You've only been here two years and already you've qualified for the Olympic Games and you'll probably go on and win the gold medal. I've been doing this all my life, scratching a living, but you just rock up and everything comes your way.'

I was really too stunned to give much of a retort. So I didn't counter that it wasn't as if I had been exempt from achieving qualifying times. Nor had I had some kind of free ride or easy route. I'd worked incredibly hard to get back into sport after my accident, and I had put in as much effort as anyone could have in completing the three Hawaii races and the Channel swim. And ultimately, I would have swapped everything I had achieved just to get my legs back and go for a run. What easy ride were they talking about exactly? Clearly, jealousy and insecurity were behind the outburst. I recognised that intellectually, but it still wounded me.

Later that night I went to my room, laid my head on my pillow and felt tears well in my eyes. Not, as you might expect, because of the confrontation, but because it triggered something inside me. Something that I usually kept so well buried that, for the most part, I never knew it was there. In the silence of my room, I surprised myself by longing for my birth mother, Avril, who'd left me 30 years earlier when she committed suicide. Where are you, Mum? You should be here, you should be part of this, I thought.

In that moment I was angry she'd taken her own life and abandoned me. It had left a void in my heart that had never been filled. I felt hollow and—apart from Paul Nunnari and a few others in my new field—I felt totally alone. I longed for my family and friends and most of all I wanted my mother Avril. I was angry at her and longed for her all at the same time. I wanted her to pick me up and share this moment of supposed joy with me.

About 1am I found a payphone and repeatedly called Australia. I spoke to Dad and Mum (Anne), I spoke to my coach, Jenni (commitments with the Australian Paralympic Committee had kept her away), and I even spoke to Michelle. I was yearning for a connection to home. At every other time in my life when I'd succeeded at a sporting level I'd been able to share the moment with a loved one. In Switzerland, cloistered within the Paralympic squad, I was adrift from everyone I cared about.

There is, of course, that quite persuasive idea that the main reason I strove to succeed in the sporting arena was simply to be loved. It had always served me well in capturing attention for myself, even as early as my time in foster care, when Enid Kerr remembered me jumping higher and running faster than anyone else. Winning things succeeded in attracting people to me, and so reinforced that behaviour.

It's a convincing argument but I'm sure there's more to it than just that, things I'm still trying to fully understand. In any case, there I was in Switzerland, having just qualified for the Olympic Games against all realistic expectations, and there was no one giving me what I craved.

No wonder I thought of my mum.

THE BUILD-UP TO BOTH THE OLYMPIC AND PARALYMPIC GAMES was incredible. Sydney buzzed with anticipation, and both torch relays—defying the cynics' expectations—attracted thousands upon thousands of spectators.

I'd been asked to carry the Olympic torch in my local area and it was an honour I accepted in a heartbeat. My duty was to pick up the torch on the Penrith side of the Victoria Bridge and take it about 1 kilometre, handing it over in Nepean Avenue which, coincidentally, was the street in which I lived.

I began the celebrations with a barbecue lunch at my house, sharing my excitement with a number of my neighbours, as well as Mum and Dad, Johnno and Gail and their kids, Marion and her husband-to-be Kerry, and Ian Morgan, who'd helped me prepare for the Channel.

After lunch I drove to nearby Jamison Park, where the day's other torch bearers were gathering. Among them was Kane Towns, the 21-year-old son of Ched, with whom I'd done all that swimming work years earlier. It was Kane's job to receive the torch at the end of the day and light a small cauldron in the park, which would stay alight until the relay began again in the morning. Kane was chosen partly to honour his father, Ched, who, tragically, had died from a heart attack while mountain climbing in the Himalayas. While I had been very sad when I heard the news, I couldn't help but think it was typical of Ched to go out like that, living life to the full.

It seemed hardly any time until it was my turn. The preceding runner approached me and as instructed, I switched on the gas cylinder hidden within the elegantly curved torch designed to emulate the sails of the Opera House. With arms raised, we 'kissed torches', and his lit torch ignited mine.

When I set off I was stunned by the size and response of the crowd, which included, I noticed with delight, a beaming Dr Gabrael, the GP who had been so insistent the accident would not be the end for me. Spectators were lining the street, standing on brick fences, and grasping the tops of street signs they'd shimmied up to get a better view. I held the torch aloft again, triggering a great roar. Just to make sure it wasn't a coincidence, I raised it again and another great cheer came from the crowd. This Olympic torch has some power, I thought.

I had, as was the protocol among all torch-bearers, a support runner, a lovely young girl who, like me, was simply caught up in the joy and spirit of the occasion. Feeling her excitement, I couldn't not let her share in the moment, so I passed her the torch to carry for a while (wondering, with a smile, if I'd have to prise her fingers apart to get it back) and her eyes lit up. I think, given the chance, she could have held that torch aloft until the Games had come and gone.

ON THE DAY OF THE OLYMPIC OPENING CEREMONY, 15 September 2000, I checked into the athlete's village just after lunch and was met by Australian Olympic Committee president John Coates and Australian swimming hero Dawn Fraser. Both wished me the best and Dawn gave me a peck on the cheek and told me to enjoy the experience. It was a worthwhile reminder, since it's easy to lose perspective when you find yourself in such an intense situation.

That afternoon, I put on the uniform the Australian Olympic team would wear for the ceremony. With green canvas pants, a yellow short-sleeved shirt and a terracotta-coloured jacket in a typically bold Mambo design, it was not the sort of thing I'd wear to the movies. But it was colourful and striking and perfect for the occasion. We were also supplied with clear plastic bags which we were asked to use as ponchos when we were making the short trip from the village to the Superdome—where all the competitors from around the world would await their call into the adjacent Olympic Stadium—because clouds had gathered threateningly above.

Thousands of the best athletes in the world were under the Super-dome's roof and jumping out of their skins with excitement. Even so, I can't imagine anyone there was as thrilled as I was. This was something I would never have dared dream about, but here I was, surrounded by the world's elite. I remarked as much to champion runner and Aussie favourite Cathy Freeman, whom I'd met a few times through our mutual connection to Nike.

Eventually, as the opening ceremony got underway, athletes began filing out behind their country's flag bearer. As the host nation, we were last,

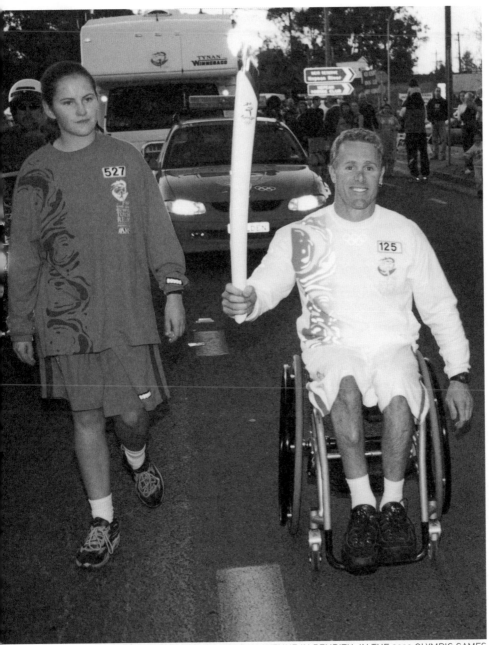

NEARING MY HOME STREET, NEPEAN AVENUE IN PENRITH, IN THE 2000 OLYMPIC GAMES
TORCH RELAY. NEVER MIND THE PROTOCOL, I COULDN'T RESIST GIVING MY
SOON-TO-BE-DELIGHTED SUPPORT RUNNER A TURN WITH THE TORCH

which only increased our anticipation. Basketballer and five-time Olympian Andrew Gaze, Australia's flag bearer, led the team out, beginning with the female contingent. Then came Kurt Fearnley and me (Kurt had landed a spot in the 1500-metre race when one of the finalists had to withdraw; he was the next fastest qualifier), leading out the men.

Outside the stadium, the walls of which towered above us, the noise was incredible. Then we were ushered down a tunnel and towards the intense light and sound. When I wheeled into the arena with the team and prepared to circle the track, the crowd of 110,000 erupted, raising the hairs on my arms and covering me with goose pimples. People seated near the track banged the advertising sidings, creating a deafening thunder. And the camera flashes: it was like being adrift in a constellation. I turned to Kurt and exclaimed, 'How good is this?'. We had the best seats in the house (literally), we were sharing the stage with the greatest athletes in the world, and billions were watching on television. If I could have drawn out that lap to last a lifetime, I would have. This wasn't one of those moments lost on me at the time; one of those moments I'd appreciate more when it had a chance to sink in. The pleasure the opening ceremony gave me was immediate. Bring on the race, I said to myself. If I could win a medal—and why not a gold?—just image how I'd feel then.

As we settled in our spot in the middle of the arena I found myself next to kayak champion Clint Robinson and, just at that moment, we both noticed Cathy Freeman slip away from the team. We gave each other a knowing look—the details of how the ceremony would unfold were a tightly guarded secret, but we figured she was leaving for a purpose, not because she'd left the iron on at home. Sure enough, heralded by Australian Olympic legends Dawn Fraser, Betty Cuthbert, Shirley Strickland de la Hunty, Raelene Boyle, Shane Gould and Debbie Flintoff-King, Cathy appeared in her memorable silver suit to light the Olympic cauldron.

Like everyone else, my heart was in my mouth when the cauldron stalled on its watery journey up to the roof of the stadium, but the end result was perfect, and it was almost as if the moment had been planned to crank the tension up another notch.

It was an incredible evening.

After the opening ceremony I went back to Penrith still on cloud nine. I lived only a short drive from the Olympic precinct and I felt the most comfortable environment in which to prepare for the race of my life was at home, surrounded by friends and a familiar routine. It's a luxury enjoyed by few athletes at the Olympics.

Thirteen days later—days in which the success of the Games was apparent to the world—my day arrived: Thursday, 28 September 2000. Although my race was not until 7pm, I went to the Olympic village around lunchtime to give myself plenty of time to prepare. In the food hall I ran into Herb Elliott, the great Australian 1500-metre runner who, when he retired as a 22-year-old, had never lost a race. A multiple world record holder and an Olympic gold medallist (in Rome, in 1960), Herb was one of my idols. It was thrilling to be sitting with him, both of us eating banana sandwiches, and listening to his advice which, as it happened, mirrored my own simple, but so far effective, tactics.

'Get in front and stay there,' said Herb, cutting to the chase.

Back in the room I was sharing with Kurt, I did my best to relax and keep my mind occupied, so I wouldn't spend too much time dwelling on what was to come. Apart from a little light stretching I did nothing but listen to music, lie down for a while, and polish my racing chair, even though it was perfectly clean. Kurt and I spoke little to each other, the fact that we were competitors outweighing our shared nationality.

A couple of hours before the race I went to the warm-up track adjoining the stadium. On a gorgeous, clear spring evening, it was abuzz with athletes warming down or warming up for races, including some of the men I'd be racing in a matter of hours, who were doing half-paced laps in their racing chairs.

I joined them, putting myself through a series of easy exercises without ever extending myself or, I hoped, giving anything away. As I'd practised, I kept telling myself that I wasn't here to make up the numbers. There's always that part of you that feels like an impostor when you begin to achieve, as if someone is going to find you out and send you back into the milling crowds where you belong. This is fairly normal, but I was good at looking at my achievements objectively and allowing myself to recognise that I'd performed well in good company. I'd got here through hard work and actual results. No one picked me out of the crowd and said, 'Here, you have a go'. I'd earned this. My performances over the past year demonstrated that I was good enough to win a medal, even win gold. I had to believe that. Otherwise I may as well have not been there.

With the race imminent, there was a call for the 1500-metre wheelchair athletes to gather. After some final instructions and encouragement from Jenni, I joined the others and we made our way to a waiting room underneath the stadium. The atmosphere was tense and you could hear, even through the thick concrete, the roar of the crowd whenever a race got underway. An Olympic official looked our racing chairs over, to ensure they complied with regulations, and we were led out into the stadium.

Wheeling around towards the start line I soaked up the atmosphere, breathed deeply and told myself the moment—my moment—had arrived. To win a medal, I'd have to beat some guys I'd never beaten before. This actually relaxed me because I knew the pressure was on them, not me. I'd done well enough in past meets to know that if I pulled out the race of my life I could get on the dais. After all I'd been through in my life, nothing would stop me putting everything I had into this race. I was not in the habit of going out half-cocked only to regret it later. To beat me, my opponents would simply have to be better.

The names of the participants in the men's 1500-metre wheelchair final were then read out by the stadium announcer.

'In Lane One, representing Australia, John Maclean.' Hearing my name, the crowd went berserk. I'm not sure if many actually knew who I was but it didn't matter. I was one of them and that was the bottom line. I've never felt so proud to be Australian.

When the rest of the introductions were over (Kurt received a cheer every bit as loud as mine), a hush began to fall over the crowd and we took up our positions along the curved start line. My heart was booming in my chest like a drum. Here we go.

Bang!

You don't do a lot of thinking in the moment after the gun goes off. You simply put your head down and belt the push-rims on the wheels, trying to build momentum as quickly as possible. As I did just that the crowd roared, and I could literally feel their energy in the air. I fed on it.

By the 500-metre mark I was sitting in second place and sucking in big breaths. Over the next 500 metres I was drawn into the middle of the pack but I wasn't panicking as I still felt strong. I just told myself to stay where I was and get ready for a surge towards the final bend.

With about 350 metres remaining I was in sixth place. The tightly bunched pack was flying and we began to jostle for position to prepare for the sprint that would decide the medallists. At that point, I found myself perilously close to Ernst van Dyke from South Africa, who was on my right shoulder as we rounded the bend. I would only discover this later, when watching the replay, but when Ernst's arms were on their way back up after a push, his left elbow bumped my right forearm just as my hands were coming down to hit my push-rim. The contact was enough to cause me to completely miss the rim. Given the upper-body force a wheelchair athlete exerts on each push, my body weight continued forward and down, causing my wheelchair to unbalance.

The catastrophic effect of this was that my racing chair tipped and my world turned upside down. The collective gasp from the crowd sounded like a tyre deflating. In that instance, sprawled on the track, one of my overturned wheels still spinning around as if it didn't know my race was over, I had a sense of déjà vu. Hadn't I been in this position before?

IN THE MOMENTS AFTER THE CRASH, I was surprised at my level of calm. I told myself that I had no control over what happened in the race (won by Mexico's Saul Mendoza who, with second place-getter Claude Issorat from France, was behind me when I crashed), so why beat myself up about it? Crashes happen all the time in the fast and furious world of men's 1500 metres, although they never had to me. What's done is done.

QUALIFYING FOR THE SYDNEY 2000 OLYMPIC GAMES WAS ONE OF THE HIGHLIGHTS OF MY CAREER. HERE I'M SITTING IN FRONT OF JEFF ADAMS OF CANADA IN THE EARLY STAGES OF THE 1500-METRES FINAL AT THE SYDNEY OLYMPIC STADIUM

The pressing matter for the officials was to pick me up off the track, particularly since the decathlon's javelin event was in progress nearby. When they did help me back into my chair, I told them I wanted to continue on the last 300 metres and finish the race. This wasn't because I wanted any sympathy or consolation from the crowd, simply that I wanted to finish what I'd started, what I'd come to do. It seemed so unfulfilling to just be escorted away, leaving my personal finish line uncrossed.

The officials, doing their job, apologised but said I had to leave the track quickly, so that's what I did. Wheeling towards the exit zone, my initial easy-come-easy-go attitude was already starting to fade and the psychological impact of the crash began to really sink in. My shoulder was grazed and my pride was hurt. But I couldn't really get all precious about it; I felt I had to put on a brave face when the trackside reporter asked me the inevitable question: how was I feeling?

I didn't have the composure or inclination to tell the painful truth. I don't think I could have properly articulated how shattered I was. So I fell back on a few robotic clichés loved by athletes the world over. 'It's not the result I was looking for, but these things are part of wheelchair racing. Now I'm just looking forward to the Paralympic Games and doing the best I can.'

I slipped on a mask when all I really wanted was to get out of there and be consoled by my friends and family.

I went back to my room in the athlete's village, gathered my gear together and turned on my mobile phone. The race had ended a little more than a half-hour earlier and my voicemail was full of messages from friends who had seen my crash on television. One message was from Wally. 'Mate, that was fantastic. Can't wait to catch up.'

What does he mean by fantastic?, I thought. A gold medal would have been fantastic.

Then the phone rang. It was David Knight. Although by this time he was working and living in Hong Kong, David had flown out to watch me race and was sitting in the stadium when I crashed. 'C'mon, mate, grab your gear, we're going out,' he said. David instinctively knew what I was going through and he wasn't about to help me feel sorry for myself. His motto was to get straight back on that horse. So that evening we went to a bar in the city to talk about what had happened.

As I told him, it was a bitter disappointment. For two years I'd directed all my energies to making myself the best wheelchair racer I could possibly be and then experienced the absolute high of qualifying not only for the Paralympic Games but the Olympic Games as well. For that latter experience to end with me sprawled on the track in front of the nation with billions watching on television was humiliating. It seemed to perpetuate the rollercoaster ride I'd been on all my life and I guess I was sick of the lows.

But I also had to face the fact that my personality lends itself to highs and lows. When I want something I give it all my energy and chase it down relentlessly. This takes away any grey area. I either win or I fail. I had just failed at the highest level and it was ever so public. I was devastated.

But David (echoing the comment Jenni had made to me; comments I hadn't really been able to take in) did his best to remind me what an amazing achievement it had been just to make the Olympic final in so short a time. The odds of me doing that, given that I had made my first foray into the sport in January 1999, were very long. My victory had been making the final. The crash, David said, wasn't exactly incidental but it wasn't the end of the world.

When I got back to Penrith, my home voicemail was also full, with messages of condolence from around the globe. (A day later, my crash even made the front page of Florida's *St Petersburg Times*, thanks to my Iron-man profile in that part of the world.) The messages of support were lovely but I was in a very self-indulgent state of mind at the time. While I kept up appearances and rattled off lines like 'crashing was disappointing but no big deal' I felt very different; the axis of my world was dangerously askew.

During this period Wally called me again, as if he knew exactly how I was feeling. Hearing how I was—really hearing, despite the act I was keeping up—he gently admonished me. 'You'll get it one day,' he said, and I had absolutely no idea what he was on about. Get what?

Two weeks after the Olympic Games closed (IOC president Juan Antonio Samaranch declared it the 'best Games ever' and I think he actually meant

WHEN I CRASHED DURING THE 1500-METRES OLYMPIC FINAL, I WANTED A HOLE TO
OPEN UP BENEATH ME AND SWALLOW ME UP

UNABLE TO COMPLETE THE RACE AFTER MY OLYMPICS CRASH, I WHEELED
OFF THE TRACK PHYSICALLY AND MENTALLY SCARRED

it), the Paralympic Games were launched at the same venue. Unfortunately, I hadn't shaken off my malaise and the entire Paralympics went by in something of a daze. Many people talked up my chances (influential Sydney media personality John Laws had me as a guest on his television show before the Paralympics and was so complimentary I'm sure his viewers expected me to win a swag of medals), but my state of mind was not what it should have been.

Compounding this less-than-ideal preparation, I think I made a major error of judgment by racing so many events. While I gave each event everything I had, I couldn't help but think when it was all over that I should have just concentrated on one or two races.

The 5000 metres semifinal was the low point of my Paralympics: I was involved in another crash and was again carted off the track. Adding to the humiliation was that, after a review of the race and the incident, the judges disqualified me. The stadium announcer passed this news on to the crowd. Since I'd crashed the disqualification was redundant, but I didn't like thinking it was deemed to be my fault.

It's amazing how quickly you can fall apart if you're not really put together that well. After swimming the Channel and completing three Hawaiian Ironmans and a host of other athletic accomplishments, I had felt rock solid, and very comfortable in my skin. But after the Olympic and Paralympic Games, the earth trembled under me. Brick by brick, I felt I was crumbling. The wall I'd put around me all my life wasn't holding together any more.

With my athletic veneer having collapsed in Sydney, my means of defining myself fell away with it. That left John Maclean the man, and I had no idea who he was.

I WAS STUCK DEEP IN THIS INTROSPECTIVE MIRE when I was awarded an Order of Australia Medal for services to sport and the promotion and encouragement of junior wheelchair athletes. It was an unexpected honour and I had the pleasure of attending Government House in New South Wales

and receiving my medal from the state governor, Gordon Samuels. Dad and Mum came to Sydney for the occasion and they were particularly proud of me.

Nevertheless, it was a brief shining moment in a very dark period and, feeling directionless, I called Wally. I was in a depressive state and beyond cheering up, though my friends and family tried. I needed to speak to someone who might understand what I was going through. Being the sort of person who routinely tapped me on the heart with insightful questions, Wally seemed perfect.

Answering his phone, Wally asked me how I was. I admitted I wasn't great and said I needed to speak to someone about it. It was the first time I'd acknowledged aloud that I was not the person I wanted to be. It was disconcerting to admit that. As important as sport had been to me, it was not everything. There was more to life. I was craving something that sport couldn't give me, win or lose.

Wally suggested I meet with Maurie Raynor—though Wally referred to him as Moses. Maurie was a mentor and former employer of Wally's and

Wally said he had an innate ability to see to the heart of a matter and the heart of a person. There's a saying that the master comes when the student is ready and I was ready. So Wally did the leg-work, called Maurie and arranged a meeting.

Maurie was recently out of hospital and convalescing at his home in Pottsville, northern New South Wales, when, knotted with apprehension, I went to see him. Bone cancer had him in its grip and Maurie didn't have long to live. 'John,' he said, 'I'm dying and I'm incapable of bullshit, so let's get on with it.'

How's that for an introduction?

I then went on to spill my soul to Maurie and to fill him in on my life's journey, culminating in my current state of confusion and sense of being untethered.

Maurie blew apart any complacency I may have had with his next comment.

'The best thing that ever happened to you was getting hit by that truck.'

I felt somewhat stunned by that, but Maurie wasn't finished. 'The next best thing that happened to you was crashing at the Olympics. Maybe that will make you realise that life doesn't revolve around John Maclean.'

As Maurie explained, my constant goal-setting was my way of finding myself, but it was flawed. All the answers I was looking for were not wrapped up in some highway or body of water or on an athletics track. Despite everything I'd done, he said, he could see I still didn't love myself and that I found it very hard to let others love me, particularly women. Too many times in my life I'd been with wonderful women but each time I kept them at arm's length, refusing to let them in. That was all tied in with the suicide of my mother, Maurie suggested. The last woman I'd truly and instinctively opened my heart to had abandoned me.

Maurie went on to tell me that the masks I'd worn throughout my life had served a vital purpose—as had my use of sport to get my life together after the accident—but they'd hindered me as well. He was right. Intuitively, I had known all of this. But I'd never admitted it to myself, nor had anyone else ever confronted me with it.

I ended up spending the weekend with Maurie and his wife, Gwen. I slept at their home and had my meals cooked for me. And all the while, Maurie, as ill as he was, would find time to speak with me and together we'd peel away a few more layers and try to take an objective look at my life, how I was handling it, and where it needed work.

It was time to reinvent myself all over again.

13 NEW DIRECTIONS

MAURIE'S MESSAGE WAS THE ONE THAT GOT THROUGH TO ME, but he wasn't the first person to tell me to open my eyes. After I'd supported David Knight's Channel swim, I had the honour of meeting his grandmother, Margaret, at a Sydney nursing home. David and I went to her room, where she was lying in bed, covered by a colourful knitted blanket. David woke her gently and she soon spotted me and attempted to make conversation.

'Has David ever told you about his friend who swam the English Channel?' she asked.

'This is him, Gran,' David replied.

Her eyes lit up and she beckoned me over.

David had obviously explained my story to her—and his strong connection to me—and I suppose she felt like she knew me so she gave me a hug, though I dwarfed her tiny frail frame.

Not long after I was to see her again. Sitting in a dining hall among the nursing home's other residents, she welcomed me with a hug but this time she didn't release me immediately. She had something to say. 'You've done some amazing things but it's time to get on with the rest of your life,' she said, stopping me in my tracks.

Where did that come from?, I wondered. Her unheralded comment hit me like a punch through a boxer's defences and I was too stunned to reply to her. This is it, mate, I said to myself. Get the lesson.

But I didn't, quite. It took a very public crash two years later before it really sank in.

FOLLOWING THE DISAPPOINTMENT of the Olympic and Paralympic Games, I found that simply being a professional athlete was no longer enough. After my weekend with Maurie I spent a lot of time contemplating how self-obsessed I'd been for so long. Everything I'd done since getting out of hospital had been, by and large, about me. And why not? I'd wanted to rebuild my life and make the most of myself despite a shattering accident. While I acknowledged there wasn't anything intrinsically wrong with this, I had never properly considered that to be the man I wanted to be required me to do more than tackle one physical challenge after another.

Succeeding in Ironman, swimming the Channel and competing in wheelchair racing had been vital for me to reclaim a sense of self-worth that had been lost in the accident (and before that, during my childhood). Clearly, however, there was more to my self-realisation than could be gained solely through sport. Had I been better rounded, with a durable self-esteem built on a good foundation, I think I would have handled my disappointments at both Games much better.

Perhaps I was being a little hard on myself since, through my Hawaii adventures and, particularly, my Channel swim, I had sincerely wanted my efforts to show children in wheelchairs that their lives weren't limited, as they might sometimes think. By seeing me conquer my condition, I hoped I could motivate them to do the same, to throw themselves into life, as I said often in interviews. Nevertheless, my primary motivation all this time was personal.

With these realisations seeping in, I found myself wondering what I was supposed to do now—the very question I had always worked so hard to avoid. The answer I came upon was not to give away everything I knew and everything I was best at (after all, I still needed to make a living and sport was my job), but to broaden my focus so that it looked outwards just as much as it looked within.

After my time with Maurie, which in retrospect sped me to a conclusion I think I was always headed towards, it seemed it was time to give something back. Something tangible.

Since my accident I had received so much generous help, support and love, and so many well wishes. People had shaken my hand on the street or taken me into their homes and hearts. This was instrumental in helping me bounce back from the accident that had nearly taken my life.

But now it felt as though I'd had a good run and I should repay my debt. Not necessarily to those who helped me specifically, but to the community. There's a movie I like called *Pay It Forward* and I think of its simple premise whenever I try to articulate what I wanted to do. Essentially, in the film, a child performs a good deed for someone else with no chance of personal gain. The recipient of that good deed is prompted to do something similar for someone else. And so on. (Paying a good deed forward, as opposed to paying it back.) It is simplistic, but it explores the notion that from one selfless gesture can come a lot of good.

These days, I've come to think that to live a happy and fulfilling life we need to find contentment and worth within ourselves, our family, our work and our community. To have one without the others can never be completely satisfying.

THE FIRST BUILDING BLOCK IN THIS NEW FUTURE I was forging for myself had actually been laid two years before. In 1998, when I was preparing to swim the Channel, Nike had solidified our relationship and offered me $20,000 to give to the charity of my choice. For a while the money burnt a hole in my pocket, as I debated which charity to donate it to.

In the end, because I felt it would be best to know directly where the funds went, I decided to establish my own benevolent organisation: the John Maclean Foundation.

The Foundation was launched later that year under the auspices of the New South Wales Wheelchair Sports Association (NSWWSA), of which I was a member. It was my intention that the Foundation would aim to assist, at a grassroots level, one boy and one girl each year who were having difficulty pursuing their sport because they couldn't afford specialised equipment. The NSWWSA would identify the children in particular need and then, at an annual presentation night, I would give them a cheque to purchase a wheelchair designed for their specific sport, such as tennis, basketball or athletics.

That's how the Foundation had worked for a couple of years and I was happy enough with that. It always delighted me to attend these presentation nights and see the thrill on the kids' faces—and the relief on their parents' faces—when I gave them their cheques. It reminded me of the delight I had always felt as a child when receiving gifts from someone I looked up to. I remember when I was 16 and Dad came home after a day working as a strapper with the Penrith Panthers football club with a pair of football boots given to me by one of the first-grade stars. Call me Cinderella, but they fitted perfectly, and I can recall the chest-filling pleasure wearing those boots gave me. To have the chance to spark that kind of feeling in a child was an exciting privilege.

Until my meeting with Maurie Raynor, that's how things stayed in terms of the Foundation: low key and low maintenance. But my chat with Maurie—who, sadly, succumbed to bone cancer in 2001—gave me the impetus to focus more on the Foundation and, ultimately, to launch it on a national scale.

My first idea was to handcycle around Australia to raise funds and increase the profile of the Foundation. Early in 2001, I floated the idea with Pat Farmer, one of Australia's most renowned ultra-distance runners, and a prolific charity fundraiser. Pat has run across the baking hot Simpson Desert in central Australia, and he's run right across the United States, but his most significant achievement was running around his own country—

following the coast, in effect—in the lead-up to the centenary of Australian Federation. He covered about 14,500 kilometres in 7 months.

Pat wasn't sold on my idea, reasoning that, due to Australia's size and relatively small population, I'd spend most of my time cycling through sparsely populated areas where, as he'd found, I'd be lucky to see a soul, let alone make any money or get exposure for the Foundation. Besides which, he said, around the Top End, where road trains barrel down the highways like cyclones, I'd risk getting run down. It would be best, he suggested, to undertake my fundraising cycle down the Australian east coast, where most of the country's population lives.

The more I thought about it the more sense this made and soon, after consultation with the Foundation's board members, I had decided that in 2002 I would handcycle 2002 kilometres, from Brisbane to Melbourne, under the banner K4K, as in 'kilometres for kids'.

With only a little more than 12 months until we planned to set off from Brisbane, there was much to organise, so I put together a team to make it happen, including Steve Plakotaris (who became the Foundation's executive director), and Trent Taylor, formerly with the NSWWSA, who became the K4K's road manager. Together we'd contact sponsors, councils, media, community groups and anyone else we thought could help make the ride a success.

From this point on, the John Maclean Foundation became my priority.

MIDWAY THROUGH 2001, as planning for the K4K was gathering speed, I was asked, much to my surprise, to participate in the famous Sydney to Hobart yacht race. The historic, 630-nautical-mile race (first held in 1945) is an institution in Australia. Its start, in Sydney Harbour on 26 December, is always spectacular and draws thousands of spectators to the foreshore and many more to the water. As the yachts head through the harbour and towards the Sydney Heads out to sea, a flotilla of spectator craft follows. Once through the Heads the race is well and truly on and sails fill for the long run to Tasmania.

The yachts' passage down the east coast of Australia can be difficult, but traditionally it's when the fleet has to cross Bass Strait, which separates Tasmania from the Australian mainland, that boats can run into wild weather. In 1998 alone, six men were drowned after huge storms slammed the fleet.

The offer to take part in the race came from computer company Aspect, which sponsored a boat by the same name. The boat's slogan was 'Sailors With disAbilities'. I was still uncomfortable with the 'disabled' tag, no matter how cleverly it was used, but the offer was attractive, primarily because I could use my participation to generate publicity for the Foundation and flag the K4K ride in the media.

I met up with *Aspect*'s skipper, David Pescud, and we discussed my possible involvement in the race. The straight-talking skipper said he'd like to have me on board because I'd add value in terms of generating exposure for the boat, whether as an active or non-active crew member. I hated the idea of just being a passenger, and said if I didn't have a useful role I couldn't accept.

Once that was established, I was invited on a sail through the Heads to see how I'd handle the conditions. In other words, the skipper wanted to see if I'd go green. So one brilliant winter's day I took my place on the 54-foot (16.5-metre) yacht and we skipped across the harbour and through the Heads, where the conditions inevitably become rougher. Thankfully, I didn't experience any seasickness despite the buffeting the yacht took. After my experiences on the tumultuous Channel, I had suspected I was one of the lucky ones who tend not to get seasick, but it was nice to confirm it.

In the weeks and months following that test run I was often aboard when *Aspect* took runs up the north coast of Australia, sometimes at night, which was a novel experience. I was new to sailing and I wanted to learn everything I could in the short time available. I was like a sponge, soaking up any knowledge that I could coax out of the crew.

Since I wanted to make a contribution, it was decided that the perfect job for me would be as a grinder. It's the grinder's job to winch in the mainsail after it has been let out to make the most of the conditions.

Considering the size of the mainsail and the fact that it is 'heavy' with wind this is no easy feat, requiring considerable strength.

After all my handcycling, I was well suited to the grinder. Located near the main mast, the grinder is essentially a winch—not unlike the cranks on a bicycle—which I would have to 'pedal' with my arms to drag the sail in. When that became too difficult I would reverse the direction of my winching, which takes the grinder down a gear, making things easier.

Obviously the deck of a yacht is not the most stable place, and holes were drilled into the deck so we could strap my wheelchair into place, while I secured myself to the grinder with a device not unlike a seat belt. That way, I wouldn't go rolling away when I was needed most.

WORKING THE GRINDER WITH KIM JAGGER (LEFT) AND MARK THOMPSON (CENTRE) AS OUR
SYDNEY-TO-HOBART YACHT *ASPECT* RACES ALONG TASMANIA'S EAST COAST EN ROUTE TO HOBART

AMID MY PREPARATIONS FOR THE SYDNEY TO HOBART and the continual work being done to get the K4K up to speed, I was becoming more active in putting myself forward as a corporate speaker, which was now my sole source of income. After engagements in Australia, and even a few in the United States, I was learning to be more selective with my story and to better tailor it to a wide range of clients.

Tony Garnett was instrumental in helping me launch this career path. So was Tony Doherty, a Melbourne real estate professional to whom Tony G had introduced me back in 1997 when I gave that talk at Parramatta Leagues Club. Tony D essentially took over where Tony G left off. I remember returning to my table at the conclusion of that talk only to have Tony Doherty, seated next to me, tell me, 'That was pretty ordinary.'

His tongue was in his cheek but I liked his boldness. While he was joking in one way, as a result of his guidance and influence, he helped me to think about public speaking for a living. He told me he had enjoyed my talk but if I didn't want to be a one-shot wonder I would need to tailor my message to different audiences. He said I had the raw talent and obviously an interesting story but that I needed to develop both.

Tony showed his faith in my ability to do that by booking me for his business's annual conference on Queensland's Gold Coast in 1998. After much tutoring from him, that presentation was a success and we've remained close since. In 1999 I had occasion to help him in return. Tony was a former rugby union player with Eastwood in Sydney, and Eastwood were playing in the grand final that year. Despite having been in the Sydney rugby competition for 52 years, the club had never won a premiership and Tony had this idea that I could speak to the team at training the week before the game and inspire them to reach heights the club had never reached before.

It took him some effort to convince John McKee, the team's coach (whom he didn't know and called out of the blue), but Tony was persistent and the coach could tell that this former player just wanted the best for the team. So it was set.

When I arrived at the training session a few days before the big game, one of the team's trainers came over and introduced himself. In a more-or-less throwaway line, he told me there were old Eastwood players sitting in nursing homes who would die happy knowing that the 'Woodies' had finally won a premiership. The image touched me.

Eventually it was time to speak to the players and I told them a little about myself, concentrating on themes of perseverance and creating your own legacy. Recalling what the trainer had told me, I let them know that while winning the grand final would be an incredible achievement for them (and create for them a lasting memory that could never be taken away, no matter what happened in the future), it would also be a special gift to all the people who'd played and been part of the club in decades past.

'This is your time,' I told them. 'Go and get it.'

My talk seemed to hit the mark and the team captain thanked me, announced that I was officially a member of the team, invited me to the grand final and requested my presence in the team dressing-room before the game.

On grand final day I wore a dress shirt I'd been given featuring the club's insignia. Sitting on the sideline I rode every play in the game, willing the team to victory. Tony was there too, having flown up from Melbourne, and there can't have been too many more delighted than him when Eastwood got up to win 34–17 against Sydney University.

As the jubilant team began a lap of honour, I saw that the Eastwood trainer sitting next to me on the bench had tears running down his cheeks. I remembered what he'd said to me at training during the week. 'What are you doing here?' I asked him. 'Get up and join the players. You've been waiting for this all your life. You're as much a part of this club as anyone. Go and enjoy the moment.'

The following day, after a boisterous night celebrating at the clubhouse, Tony left, worse for wear, but sporting the shirt I'd been given by the club—I'd thought he'd appreciate it even more than me.

That same year I was invited to Tony's 40th birthday in Melbourne, but unfortunately I couldn't go. I'd been notified that I'd been awarded an Australian Sports Medal and that Prime Minister John Howard was to present me with the medal in Sydney on the same evening as Tony's party.

I called to apologise and let Tony know why I couldn't make it. But after hanging up I just didn't feel right.

With no disrespect to the prime minister (and not intending to downplay my delight at being recognised for the award), I decided it was more important for me to go to my mate's 40th. I'd been travelling a lot and the more time I spent away from home, family and friends, the more their importance struck home to me. The thought of being at an awards evening while a close friend was elsewhere celebrating a major milestone was too much.

Soon after I was telephoned by the PM's office enquiring about my attendance at the awards, for which I hadn't yet replied. 'Sorry,' I said, 'I can't make it. Can you send it in the post?'. They did.

I attended Tony's birthday and never regretted it for a second. How often had Tony and people like him made sacrifices for me?

ON CHRISTMAS DAY 2001, the day before the Sydney to Hobart race, I was at Johnno's house in Sydney's west for a roast lunch with his family. This despite the fact that it was one of those baking hot summer days in Sydney when a westerly wind blows in off the desert bringing with it squadrons of flies and prime conditions for bushfires.

Johnno's place backed onto a ridge of bush but, while spot fires were being fought by bushfire brigades in the area, it didn't seem we'd be in any danger. However, as the day progressed and the sky turned a violent orange, that opinion changed. The fires that had seemed so far away were now approaching the house. By the afternoon, the sky was thick with smoke, the heat had intensified and the wind picked up. Burning embers had set alight piles of dead wood on land plots adjoining Johnno's own block, and the flames were leaping 10 metres high.

In one of my most memorable Christmas Day experiences ever, I then found myself with Johnno, wet tea towels covering our faces, putting out spot fires on his land and in the guttering of his house, where leaf litter was igniting. Considering we just had garden hoses, we were lucky the fire didn't change direction. Instead, it just roared through the vacant lot next door. Though the tops of the pine trees surrounding Johnno's home were scorched and his yard was peppered with smouldering black smudges, the danger passed us by.

That was all fresh in my mind the following morning when I was boarding *Aspect* for the Sydney to Hobart. Bushfires were now ringing Sydney and the dark smoke could be seen sweeping over the city. It was a surreal sight.

Fortunately, from a firefighting perspective, the wind was reasonably calm on the morning of the race. From a sailing standpoint, however, this was not ideal and it meant the fleet didn't exactly explode into action when the gun fired to get us underway. It was a slow if picturesque run to the Sydney Heads, where we'd turn right and head for Hobart.

Even once we breached the Heads the wind remained gentle, and we experienced the odd sensation of being out at sea yet still brushing away flies that had been blown out of their orbit by the previous day's westerlies. But soon the wind began to pick up, allowing us to let out more sail and begin our long run south.

It took us the best part of four days to get to Hobart and it was an experience I'll never forget. Working on a four-hours-on, four-hours-off basis, it was physically tough at times, but being a part of such a great crew and unique experience made it all worthwhile. Then there were the gorgeous sunsets, and the long beautiful nights, where, away from the lights of the mainland, the stars and the moon leap out at you and put you in your place.

More than that, I'd always been someone who had his phone on. Someone who was always busy and had people around me. This was driven home particularly during our crossing of Bass Strait when, off duty, I was sitting on the side of the yacht, with my harness on and my feet slung overboard, staring out at the horizon in complete silence. It was beautiful and incredibly invigorating. I vowed that when I got home I'd try to make more time for myself away from life's distractions.

Bass Strait was relatively kind to the 2001 fleet. It did get woolly at times for us, with the boat heeling steeply on a number of occasions, but it was nothing the skipper and the crew couldn't handle. Nevertheless, it was a good feeling, at around 3am, to be sailing up the Derwent River in Hobart towards the finish line. As memorable as it had been, it was hardly a luxurious ride and we were all longing to go to our respective homes and give our big, wide beds some serious attention.

14 THE LONG ROAD

AFTER COMPLETING THE SYDNEY TO HOBART, my full attention turned to the K4K, which was scheduled to commence on 1 June 2002. Such a project required meticulous planning. It wasn't simply a case of setting off from Brisbane and hoping for the best. My team and I left nothing to chance.

In preparation for the ride, Steve, Trent and I did a few reconnaissance trips to various towns along the route. As well as liaising with sponsors, local governments, police and media, we spoke to schools and community groups, because at the end of every day we wanted some local children in wheelchairs to join me for the final 100 metres of my ride.

The theory was that, by joining me, they would not only enjoy themselves and the atmosphere but also get a tangible, positive example of the scope for people in wheelchairs. I was fortunate enough to have had the use of my legs as a child, but I can imagine how difficult it must sometimes be for kids to motivate themselves. To many, the chair must feel like an anchor.

WITH MY BRAVE MATE JACOB RAY AND HIS COACH, JASON BATSON, MOMENTS BEFORE JACOB SWAM ACROSS THE SHOALHAVEN RIVER TO RAISE MONEY FOR CAMP QUALITY AND THE JOHN MACLEAN FOUNDATION

It doesn't help that, even today, people in wheelchairs often have great difficulty accessing such basic needs as shops, restaurants and public transport. Only by spending time in a wheelchair can you really get an idea of the logistical problems that routinely face people without full mobility.

Someone who knows a lot about that is a young boy by the name of Jacob Ray. I first met Jacob in 1993 when I was touring New South Wales as a Spinesafe lecturer and was invited to speak at a primary school in Culburra, coincidentally the same town Dad and Mum had moved to a few years earlier on the south coast.

Jacob was about five years old at the time and he was the only child in the school in a wheelchair. When I was introduced, I decided to align myself with Jacob (whose paraplegia was due to neuroblastoma, a type of cancer) and invite him to sit alongside me with his schoolmates surrounding us. I made the point to everyone of how similar Jacob and I were, as I taught them about spinal cord function and how difficult life can be when a spinal cord becomes damaged through accident.

Since then I've continued to visit Jacob whenever I'm in Culburra catching up with Dad and Mum, and I've been delighted to see him grow into a fine, positive-thinking young man—one with a wonderfully developed social conscience. I was thrilled to discover in the lead up to the K4K that Jacob, by then 10 years old, had decided to swim across the Shoalhaven River to raise money for the cancer-based charity Camp Quality and my Foundation.

Considering our history, I made sure I was in attendance the day Jacob gamely swam across the river and raised over $10,000, half of which went to the Foundation. I was incredibly proud and, to pay tribute, I decided to dedicate the first kilometre of the K4K to him.

THE NIGHT BEFORE THE K4K WAS DUE TO COMMENCE we officially launched the event on the television program *The Footy Show*. I'm sure I made a very frustrating guest because I steered every question asked of me around to the Foundation. But the exposure the interview provided for the ride was significant, and that gave us useful impetus when we set off the following morning.

What with all the negotiations and planning, I must admit I hadn't actually given much thought to the difficulty of handcycling 2002 kilometres in 30 days. It was going to be tough on my arms and shoulders, but I figured I had a good base after all my triathlons and swimming and I knew I could tough it out if need be. The benefit of a daily grind like the K4K is that, barring injury, every day becomes a training session for the following day— you get fitter and stronger as the event wears on.

That was my hope, at least, when we set off from Brisbane; me on the handcycle and a large crew (which included a few of the Foundation's board members, Ross Hutchinson, who was acting as my masseur, and my Dad) split between three support vehicles. One, driven by David Wells, would travel in front of me, while the other two would follow, all three keeping in radio contact. While this was a very different undertaking to Ironman and the Channel, I enjoyed the same feeling I had then: that I was part of a team, a cog in a bigger wheel.

Aside from rest days, a typical day during my K4K marathon began with an alarm piercing my skull at 5.45am so I could do a daily radio update on my progress. Following a big breakfast, I tried to get most of my day's cycling—sometimes as much as 140 kilometres—under my belt by early afternoon. At the end of each day's ride, I'd be met by local kids in wheelchairs. After greeting them all, I'd get out of my handcycle and into my day chair, so that together we could wheel the last section of the day's ride, which always concluded through a finishing chute my crew had set up earlier. Usually, families and friends of the children and local supporters would be waiting there to cheer us home. For me, this was the highlight of each day. It made all the aches and pains worthwhile and it convinced me of the wisdom of the undertaking.

After arriving at the finish, we were often invited to a warm mayoral function before we'd all slip away and check into whatever accommodation we had arranged. While my equipment and the vehicles were readied for the following day, I'd have a soak in the bath, soothing the fatigue and stiffness in my body.

Late in the afternoon the whole team would kick the can around town, by which I mean we'd infiltrate every mall, shop, club, pub and government office we could to try and rustle up donations for the Foundation. The emotional impact of the wheelchair on potential donors helped enormously, as shown by the amount of money I was able to collect compared to the others, who would often return to base with little in their buckets.

Though exhausted by this stage of the day, we usually had a few more responsibilities to attend to, such as a fundraising function at a local chamber of commerce, or a Rotary group, Lions Club or somewhere similar. At each of these functions I'd give a talk about my experiences with paraplegia, the objectives of the John Maclean Foundation, and my wish to see children in wheelchairs given the opportunity, through encouragement and adequate equipment, to improve the quality of their life. And, more importantly, for them to be seen as equal.

Once we returned to the hotel after the evening function we'd literally count our coins so they could be banked the next day. If we were lucky we'd be in bed by 10.45pm. I'm not a night owl and usually by then, with a full day's exercise and activity behind me, I resembled the walking (or is that wheeling?) dead.

While meeting the kids at the end of every ride was the daily highlight of the K4K, there were many other memorable moments. Our welcome and reception in Ballina, in northern New South Wales, sticks in my mind. We had come across from Lismore that day and it had been a lazy 50-kilometre ride through the beautiful hills of Alstonville and down to the coast. That night the Ballina Lions Club put on a wonderful barbecue for us and we were told the fire brigade would escort us out of town in the morning following a breakfast put on by the ladies from the Lions Club.

Up at the crack of dawn we readied our gear and welcomed the ladies, who'd been up since 4am baking. Assuming there'd be breakfast fare such as Danish pastries, muffins and bacon and eggs, we were somewhat surprised to find they'd made us an enormous batch of scones topped with curried egg. Curried egg is not a regular part of my diet and I was very hesitant about eating it first thing in the morning. So were the others, but the lovely ladies had gone to a lot of trouble so everyone, particularly David, threw caution to the wind.

I thought I was doing very well to avoid the delicacy until one of our hosts, who had been keeping an eye on me, noticed that the scones were fast disappearing and I hadn't had one. I think she thought I was being polite and letting the others get their fill before I got stuck in. So she put some aside for me, and what could I do after that but munch away and smile? The ladies were chuffed that we finished off their handiwork, though I dare say they wouldn't have been as happy had they accompanied us on the day's trip when we were given—or gave—constant reminders of those scones. Not being confined to a vehicle, thankfully I escaped most of the trouble.

Another day, not far from Ballina—on a smooth downhill stretch of road between Taree and Forster—I experienced a kind of symbolic moment, much to the horror of those in my support vehicles.

On this particular day I was cycling about an inch from the rear of the lead vehicle, whose hatch door was open, as usual, so I could listen to blues music blasting out from the speakers angled for my benefit. By tucking in so close behind the vehicle, the wind resistance was reduced enormously and there was a sensation of being pulled along. In cycling it's known as drafting.

As we started heading down the hill, a kind of reckless joy possessed me and I kept cranking the pedals, literally forcing David—who could see me through the rear-vision mirror—with nods of my head, to speed up. As the slipstream effect increased, so did my speed. If I'd moved to the side of the vehicle and into the full force of the headwind I would quite probably have lost control in an instant. But tucked in behind the car it was smooth sailing, and I was euphoric. Just as when I was running in my childhood, the sensation of speed took me out of myself.

They were getting seriously worried and angry in the lead car when I passed 100 kilometres per hour. Particularly bothered was Alex Hamill, Foundation chairman and wise head, who was in the passenger seat of the vehicle ahead of me. 'Please slow down,' Alex screamed at me. 'You've reached the hundred, so now it's time to slow down.'

At such a speed, with no protection other than a helmet, I wouldn't have fared well in a crash, but I couldn't help myself. I was cycling for the Foundation, sure, but that didn't mean I couldn't have fun, did it? Eventually, as the hill bottomed out, my speed began to drop and Alex was able to remind me of my responsibility to get to Melbourne in one piece.

His concern was well placed, as I proved a few days later during a 130-kilometre leg between Bulahdelah, on the mid-north coast of New South Wales, and Newcastle. That day we were scheduled to meet a group of cyclists representing the Westpac Rescue Helicopter Service, which had been supporting the ride. They were due to meet us at Raymond Terrace and ride the rest of the leg with us.

But, about 20 kilometres into the ride, our plans were thrown into disarray. I was happily cycling through a range of hills on a granulated, pot-holed road that had seen better days. When I found myself heading downhill, once again the child in me couldn't resist giving it everything. Halfway down one hill, the rear axle on my handcycle snapped in two and

DRIVEN BY A PURPOSE BIGGER THAN ME, THE FOUNDATION'S 2002-KILOMETRE K4K CYCLE BETWEEN
BRISBANE AND MELBOURNE RAISED ABOUT $400,000 FOR CHILDREN IN WHEELCHAIRS

the cycle caved in, sending me into a frightening slide, accompanied by a soundtrack of screeching metal on bitumen. I fought to pull my body away from the road but I couldn't hold myself up for long and I painfully skidded to a stop on my left side, still in the collapsed handcycle.

The accident surprised the support vehicle behind me and it was forced to jam on the brakes. It missed running me down by a matter of inches. While the crew got our vehicles to the side of the road and attempted to divert traffic around the accident, David, who worked as a paramedic, attended to me.

The main problem, one I was familiar with, was road rash. It looked as though someone had taken a cheese grater to my entire left side. Fortunately I hadn't broken anything except my pride and my handcycle. Nevertheless, I was worse for wear and the collective decision was that I be driven to the town of Karuah, about 40 kilometres south. There my team had arranged for an ambulance to meet us and look me over.

Once I'd been seen to in Karuah, and it was determined that I didn't need any further treatment, I decided to continue on my spare handcycle, the one that had taken me through Hawaii in 1997. While the snapped axle wasn't exactly my fault, I felt somewhat responsible because I was clearly going too fast for the conditions. I'd not only placed my own life at risk, but I'd also risked implicating my own support crew in my death had they not happened to pull up behind me. (On the other hand, imagine the publicity for the Foundation if they hadn't braked in time. Maybe not.) So, road rash or not, I felt I had to honour the commitment to meet the other cyclists. I didn't want to disappoint anyone.

Initially I was extremely tentative on the handcycle and I must have looked a sight with my left leg and arm swathed in bandages. When we reached Raymond Terrace, about 40 kilometres north of Newcastle, we were amazed to see 60 cyclists ready to join us for the final stretch. By this stage, in typical fashion, I was already forgetting about the painful lesson I'd learnt in the crash, and the larrikin within re-emerged. Travelling along in the group, I gradually increased my speed while racing behind the car. The pleasure I gained from outracing good cyclists meant that instead of staying together, we ended up spread over 3 kilometres, which kind of defeated the purpose. I just couldn't seem to help myself.

I suppose the consolation for those who may have been annoyed at my competitive behaviour was that for days to come—and particularly in the shower that night—I was in considerable pain. Even today the scars of that crash remain.

One of the highlights of the K4K was my arrival in Sydney. The Sydney City Council, aided by the police, did us a great honour by closing off one lane of the Sydney Harbour Bridge. Anyone who has travelled over this Australian icon would know that this is a very rare privilege. Not that I was alone. A huge group of cyclists—including Hans Hulsbosch, who designed the Foundation's logo—joined us for the crossing, which was filmed from a helicopter.

Once off the bridge we discovered that a lane of George Street, one of Sydney's main thoroughfares, had also been closed to traffic and we had a clear run up to the Town Hall, where we were met by the Deputy Lord Mayor and a large, boisterous crowd. Arriving in Sydney in such a spectacular fashion brought home what wonderful exposure the ride was getting. I was only halfway to Melbourne but I knew then that the ride would be successful. The John Maclean Foundation was on the map.

Dad left us in Penrith, and Johnno jumped aboard for the trip south. Days later, after passing through Canberra, the nation's capital (where Prime Minister John Howard was kind enough to meet me—I guess he didn't have a mate's birthday party on that day), we were on the home stretch. Into the rhythm of the day and enjoying each other's company considerably, it was somewhat sad to contemplate the end. As gruelling as it had been, the team had grown close in the way people often do when they share the joys and difficulties of an endurance event.

On the thirtieth day we set off for the last leg—joined by a supporter who had generously donated $5000—from Seymour, in country Victoria, to Melbourne. Australia is a nation of contrasts, and though we started the K4K in balmy weather (what passes as winter in temperate Brisbane), we were to end it in bone-creaking cold. When my early morning call went

OUTSIDE THE SYDNEY TOWN HALL DURING THE K4K I WAS JOINED BY A NUMBER OF LOCAL CHILDREN
[INCLUDING JACOB RAY, SECOND FROM RIGHT] AS WELL AS [AT REAR, FROM LEFT TO RIGHT]
HANS HULSBOSCH, FOUNDATION BOARD MEMBER PAUL APPLEBY, BRENDA HAMILL,
FOUNDATION CHAIRMAN ALEX HAMILL, SYDNEY LORD MAYOR LUCY TURNBULL, AND GRAEME MACLEAN

through to the radio station it was about 2 degrees Celsius, pouring with rain and blowing a gale. With those conditions, it was comforting to know we'd already arranged a police escort into Melbourne.

The first part of this final leg was a strain. The rain and wind were bad enough but it was the cold that I found particularly hard to deal with. Despite the physical exertion, not to mention gloves and booties, I just couldn't get warm, and by the 40-kilometre mark I needed to stop, just to have a break and get out of the weather. I dare say some Antarctic explorers would scoff at my softness, but I was absolutely freezing.

Fearing hypothermia, I pulled to a halt in the outer Melbourne suburbs and Johnno helped me into the passenger seat of the lead vehicle where we cranked up the heating. I sat there for some time, thawing out, loving the fact that every shard of rain and every buffet of wind hitting the car was one less to hit me when I resumed.

Clearly I couldn't sit in the car forever, however, so it was back on the handcycle for the final stretch. Miraculously, as we got closer, the rain stopped and for the first time that day the sun came out. It reminded me of the dramatic atmosphere created when the sun broke through after my Channel swim.

Cycling down Swanston Street, right through the city centre, I was joined yet again by kids in wheelchairs. This time there were more than twenty and they pushed beside me for the final 500 metres to the Town Hall where Melbourne's Lord Mayor put on a lavish civic reception. We were met, despite the cold, by hundreds of spectators, friends and families of the kids, who gave us a rousing reception and a fitting end to what had been an eventful and (my crash aside) perfectly executed fund-raising event.

SITTING BEHIND DAVID WELLS DURING THE TOUGH OPEN-WATER MOLOKAI CHALLENGE IN HAWAII IN MAY 2005. WE RAISED $20,000 FOR THE FOUNDATION BY COMPLETING THE 55-KILOMETRE RACE

When we tallied it all up some time later, we found we'd raised about $400,000 for the Foundation and gained considerable media exposure. So successful was the ride that we soon took on other board members and attained fully fledged charitable status for the Foundation.

We changed the Foundation's focus in a way I am really happy with. We decided we needed to recognise the needs of all children in wheelchairs, not just children who are interested in sport. Having always liked the idea that the Foundation strove to help kids get out of the house and get them into life, I didn't want to confine the definition of 'life' to sport. For some kids, getting out of the house is challenge enough. So we looked at how we could help them realise a dream, no matter what form it took. It might be playing a musical instrument or learning to paint, or even having a family holiday. It might simply be helping to make their house wheelchair-friendly if their family doesn't have funds to do this.

I had changed my life's focus so it encompassed more than sport, and it was fitting that the Foundation's work now did, too.

The Foundation has really taken on a life of its own and, in the seven years since its inception, has raised more than $830,000. This includes the $20,000 raised in May 2005 when David Wells and I, competing in a two-man surf ski, contested the Molokai challenge, a punishing 55-kilometre open-water race in Hawaii. As with the K4K, I found at Molokai that I could continue to challenge myself in ways I'd enjoyed doing since I was a boy, while at the same time, instilling more purpose in these challenges by taking the focus off me.

The pleasure I've gained from seeing the Foundation develop has certainly enriched me and helped me along my personal journey.

A FEW MONTHS AFTER THE K4K, there was a very unexpected postscript to my Hawaiian adventures. Opening the mail one morning, I was stunned to read that I was to be inducted into the Ironman Triathlon World Championship Hall of Fame. I was the first non-American and the first wheelchair athlete to be granted that honour.

On the day of the induction—which took place at a hotel in Kona a few days before the 2002 Ironman—I tracked down Australian triathlete Greg Welch in his hotel. Greg won the Hawaiian Ironman in 1994 and had been a consistent performer in other years. He was an idol of mine and I felt he should be getting this honour rather than me. I wanted to tell him so. But Greg was magnanimous. 'Grab it with both hands. You deserve it,' he said generously. 'My turn will come.'

My induction into the Hall of Fame was preceded by an introduction by David Knight. It was an honour for me because not only was David an Ironman himself, he knew me as well as anyone and I loved him like a brother. His speech was very flattering as he described what he saw as my strengths. This is, in part, what David had to say:

> In 1941, Sir Winston Churchill was asked to speak to the graduating class at the Harrow School—considered then to be the future gentlemen of England. The myth is he stood before them stating that he had only twelve words for them that day.
>
> They were...
>
> 'No matter what happens in life,
>
> Never ever, ever, ever give up!'
>
> Now, everyone here is part of the Ironman family. And I would venture to suggest that all of us, in some way, recognise the sentiment behind those simple words. We've all felt the need to give up. We've all felt pain we thought we couldn't run through. We've all wondered, at some time, why we do this.
>
> But I only know one person who brings real meaning to those words.
>
> I would like to introduce you to him tonight. His name is John Maclean.
>
> Anyone here who knows John, or who has raced with him (or perhaps been passed by him), might recognise a shirt he likes to wear. It has his own logo printed on it and a few words underneath that were said to John as he struggled backwards up the hill

coming out of the old snakepit at the start of the marathon in 1995. With John's arms quivering and pain written large on his face, his best friend Johnno said, 'Keep going, mate; the pain won't last forever but the memories will'.

They are words that John chooses to live by. And they should be an inspiration to all of us.

But something tells me that John, with his usual modesty, doesn't realise quite what an inspiration he provides to all of us. I have not had a bad day since I met John Maclean, and I am now an Ironman because of him and I thank him for it every day.

His message to all of us is bigger than the one he wears on his shirt. In one way or another, we have all been faced with pain and challenges big and small. But John's message is simple ...

'No matter what happens in life,

No matter what,

Never ever, ever, ever give up!'

My acceptance speech wasn't over-elaborate. Still a little choked up by David's words, I simply tried to explain what had driven me to keep coming back to Hawaii until I got it right. I spoke about not wanting to live with regret and to be relentless when faced with challenges, whatever they may be.

'Any challenge worth overcoming is always going to be hard,' I said. 'But you've just got to keep going until you get to the finish line. The rewards will more than make up for it.'

MY LIFE TOOK ANOTHER TURN FOR THE BETTER midway through 2003 when I began seeing a beautiful woman named Rebecca. We'd first met in the lead-up to the Olympics when I was invited to talk to some members of the New South Wales Institute of Sport (NSWIS). An Olympian herself, Rebecca was a rower at the NSWIS, and I felt an instant attraction, but it would be many years, during which we occasionally saw each other at various functions, before we both had the chance to explore the possibilities of a relationship.

BEFORE EVERY HAWAIIAN IRONMAN RACE THERE IS AN OPENING CEREMONY CALLED THE PARADE OF NATIONS. DAVID KNIGHT JOINED ME IN THE OCTOBER 2003 PARADE THROUGH THE STREETS OF KONA

I remember, just before we got together, being invited to a party at her brother's place in Sydney and, to save me driving home, I was offered a bed for the night. Rebecca was in the next room and I was as nervous and excited as a teenage boy by her proximity, although I was too conscious of not putting my foot in it to make any kind of bold manoeuvre.

A week later, Rebecca had a conference in the Blue Mountains and, with me living so close by in Penrith, I offered her a place to stay—an offer she duly took up.

As I would soon discover, Rebecca not only matched my enthusiasm for sport and training (we had many a competitive cycle around Centennial Park, rain, hail or shine), but she had a disarming insight. She was the first partner to look right inside me and see that there were some truths and fears that I was keeping well hidden. 'You wear your mask really well,' she said, 'but I can see you.'

In August 2003, I invited Rebecca to join me in Prague for the Handcycling World Championships and it was shortly after returning home that Rebecca moved in with me in Penrith.

For the first time in my life I was beginning to think that there was someone with whom I could spend the rest of my life.

WITH THE LOVELY REBECCA IN PRAGUE FOR THE 2003 HANDCYCLING WORLD CHAMPIONSHIPS

15 WHATEVER MAY COME

ON THE EMOTIONAL ROLLER-COASTER THAT IS LIFE, highs don't last forever. In my case, one of my life's major lows was waiting around the corner. But, as with my Olympic crash, it wasn't without its lessons.

Early in 2004 I had what amounted to an emotional breakdown when my relationship with Rebecca ended. This was yet another failed relationship in my life, with me and my deficiencies as the common denominator. The difference with this relationship was that I had begun to learn to love in ways that had previously escaped me. That's what made it hurt even more— though I suppose you could say (and some did) that I had it coming, relationship karma being what it is.

While our relationship was far from perfect (and I was not the only one with issues to deal with, as is always the case), I honestly thought we'd be together forever. But once a small hole developed in the fabric of the relationship, it didn't take long for it to grow into something that we just couldn't mend.

Part of my problem was a lack of confidence, at least in terms of intimacy and love. That isn't surprising considering the skeletons of failed relationships I had rattling in my cupboards. It's also easy to second-guess yourself as you teeter on the edge of a longed-for commitment: what if I give her everything I have and I'm rejected? Where would that leave me?

I had made much progress after my Olympic crash and the re-evaluation that prompted, but I was still tentative about really giving myself to a woman. For one thing, I didn't quite know *how* to do that. Here was this person I was in love with and I just couldn't articulate those feelings properly to her, even though I was paid to speak for a living.

On the day Rebecca was moving out I could feel all of this welling inside me, yet I kept telling myself that I was okay, I was fine, I'd dealt with much worse in my life. I got on with wrapping glasses, packing and marking boxes and asking what she wanted and where she wanted it.

Of course this had all happened before and I had inevitable flashbacks to the time Michelle left the same house in the same fashion. I continued to tell myself to get on with it and to not feel sorry for myself (as I'd told myself time and again in the past), but my mind began to take off in directions that surprised me. And as much as I tried to reel it in, the task was beyond me.

Stretching packing tape over the closed flaps of a box, I thought of Mum's mental illness and suicide and I lamented that I'd never developed a special bond or connection with her. Surely that had something to do with what was happening now and what had happened in the past.

Before Michelle left I had, of course, thought about the fact that I hadn't quite connected with previous girlfriends, and while it was frustrating to me at the time, I didn't really try to work out what was going wrong. I certainly didn't think I had much to do with it. I just figured I hadn't met the right person. Immaturely, I'd connected love to sex, not to the act of giving in a relationship. I thought this despite the fact that a big part of me craved that very connection. I just didn't know how to go about making it. So on I went making the same mistakes over and over.

It built to a crescendo that day in 2004 as this wonderful woman walked out of my life. While the removalists were lugging her stuff out to the truck,

I sat on an outdoor lounge overlooking the pool and started crying, something I hadn't come close to doing when Michelle left because I was far less in touch with my emotions back then. The thing was, I wasn't just crying because Rebecca was leaving, though there was definitely that; I was crying for all the loss and suffering I'd felt in my life.

One memory, such as the effect of Mum's suicide, would lead to another. A backlog of painful feelings jostled to get out and, against my will, I was transported back to all the occasions on which I'd suppressed my grief, including my accident—one of the single most dramatic and defining moments in my life.

Certainly during these difficult times I'd often allowed myself a brief cry, which took the edge off the pain. But I'd capped the well prematurely and just got on with things; I'd been a brave little soldier, as Dad would say. Now it seemed every drop of grief, sorrow and sadness I'd swallowed in my life was making its way out. Where was it all coming from?, I wondered, as deep sobs racked my body. It felt as though I could have filled the pool with my tears. It was overwhelming.

Seeing me in such a state, Rebecca came out and we hugged for what seemed like half an hour. But the truck was packed, its engine was idling and she had to leave. As they had done ten years earlier when Michelle left, the garage doors closed and I was alone again.

In the days and weeks ahead my grief would keep returning. I'd be sitting in the car at traffic lights, or watching television, and it would sneak up on me and force its way out. But as time went on the tears dried up and gradually I began to feel refreshed, a different person. I won't pretend to suggest that this episode somehow completed my understanding of myself (I firmly believe this is something we have to strive for our entire lives), but it would prove to be a catharsis, a vital step in the learning process I'd begun with Maurie after the downward spiral that followed my Olympic and Paralympic Games disappointments. Although it would take a full year before I even contemplated dating again, I was washed clean with tears and began to feel better and more hopeful than I ever had before.

I'M OFTEN ASKED, in light of what I've managed to achieve since the accident, whether—if it were possible—I would give up everything I've done to go back to being John Maclean as a 22-year-old footballer who never crossed paths with that truck.

Up until a few years ago I wouldn't have hesitated. 'Yes' would have been my answer. Today, I'm not so sure. It's impossible to imagine how my life might have turned out. Perhaps I would have worked my way back into first-grade football and gone on to be a success. Perhaps I would have become a fireman, got married and had a couple of beautiful children by now, content with my lot (although this seems very unlikely given the emotional scars I was carrying around long before the accident). It's hard to compare my life to something I can only speculate about.

What I can say is that I'm a better person today because of where I've come from, the experiences I've had and the people I've met. Would I have ever known David Knight, for instance, or become close to Johnno in the way I have, or met all the other people who have touched my life if that truck had not changed the direction of my life? Would I have forged my character in the same way without the lava fields of Hawaii or the surging swell of the English Channel? Probably not.

I don't know how my life would have unfurled had I not had the accident, but I can say that my life today is enriched in a way I never would have expected when I was lying in that hospital bed. In fact, if anyone had even suggested to me then that my life would turn out to be full and rich, I wouldn't have believed them for a second, and would probably have told them where to get off in no uncertain terms. How could any good could from this, I would have thought, looking down at my shattered body.

But ending up in a wheelchair forced me to make the most of what I had and develop a view of the world that has stood me in good stead ever since. I opened myself up to new experiences and people, learning about myself in the process. It took a long time to accept myself as a paraplegic; to accept that while I got about differently to most people I wasn't different in any other way. But I got there.

ONE OF THE MOST IMPORTANT PEOPLE IN MY LIFE: MARION'S DAUGHTER, MY NIECE, ALANA, AT AGE 4 in 2004

The skin I'm in fits fine and most days I never think for one second about my accident and the lack of function in my legs. I am who I am and my days of looking back and wishing things were different are long gone.

This isn't to say that if one day science makes it possible for me to walk again I would turn down the opportunity. I hope it doesn't sound like a betrayal of my journey to self-acceptance, because I don't think it is. It's simply a reflection of the realities of the world. Having my legs back, while at the same time being the person I became without the use of them, would be incredible.

As it would be to run again like I did in my youth, leaving the world in my wake.

But I'm not holding my breath for that; it's not a salvation. I haven't put my life on hold in the past waiting for such a gift, and nothing has changed. Every day I wake up eager—to borrow a phrase—to suck the marrow out of life. I'm still playing the saxophone, I've become a voracious reader and I've even started learning to express myself by painting on canvas, which I never would have predicted. I'm passionate about the Foundation, about my four-year-old niece Alana, and the rest of my family and friends.

And I reckon, through it all, I've learned to love myself.

Having said that, I don't for a moment think I've fought my last battle, but I now feel better prepared, and more hopeful than ever before, to endure whatever comes and emerge stronger for it.

Giving up is simply not an option.

ACKNOWLEDGMENTS

I would like to thank those who saved my life, and the many others who have nurtured me and shared in my journey. This includes the medical staff at Westmead and Royal North Shore hospitals, who brought me back from the brink of death; my family, friends and mentors, who through their love and generosity of spirit have shown me that the future is brighter than I ever could have imagined; the hard-working team at the John Maclean Foundation; my ever-supportive sponsors at Gatorade, Nike, Holden, Accor, Qantas, Oakley, Invacare, Nortel, Mercedes, Panther Cycles, Pfizer, Express Data, Penrith Panthers, St Marys Rugby League Football Club, NRMA Insurance, TAB Ltd, Macquarie Bank, and the Motor Accidents Authority; and everyone at Murdoch Books who helped me put this book together, including Hazel Flynn, who with a keen, sensitive eye matched the authors together so well. Finally I'd like to thank Paul Connolly, who with sensitivity and good humour helped me explore my life's roller-coaster journey then turn our many hours of interviews into this book.

PHOTOGRAPHIC CREDITS

All photos are courtesy of John Maclean and the Maclean family with the exception of the following:

Anthony Phelps: pages 220–221, 224, 225

David Hill: pages 92–93, 134

Delly Carr: pages 90, 97, 149

Lisa Saad: pages 166, 174, 186, 252

Newspix: page 75

Penrith Rugby League Football Club: pages 60–61

Steve Snyder: page 137

The World Triathlon Corporation: pages 126, 151

Every effort has been made to contact the copyright holders and photographers concerned; if any omission has been made, Murdoch Books will be happy to correct this in future editions

WE'RE ALL REALLY EXCITED TO REACH MELBOURNE AT THE FINISH OF THE K4K RIDE IN 2002, INCLUDING JOHNNO (IN RED TOP) AND DAVID WELLS (IN GREY TOP AND BEANIE)

'the pain won't last forever but the memory will'®

In 1998, John established the John Maclean Foundation, in recognition of the generous support that he was given during his years as a professional athlete. With the original mission of helping junior wheelies to 'get into life' through sport, the foundation is now a national organisation providing assistance to Australian wheelchair users under the age of 18, regardless of whether they participate in sport or not.

John's personal mission statement is that there are 'only possibilities'. This philosophy is central to the activities of the John Maclean Foundation. With the Foundation's mission being to inspire, motivate and enable physically challenged children to live their lives to the absolute fullest, the Foundation gives practical shape to John's core belief.

John has long been a vocal and articulate advocate for the rights of children in wheelchairs. He has used his considerable motivational talents to encourage junior wheelies to chase their dreams. By conducting major fundraising activities such as the Kilometres for Kids (K4K), the John Maclean Foundation is turning little Aussie lives around.

The Foundation's prime agenda is to provide financial and equipment assistance to Australia's wheelchair kids. Each year the John Maclean Foundation awards grants to applicants on a needs basis. In 2004 alone, the John Maclean Foundation provided over $80,000 in financial and equipment assistance to junior Aussie wheelies. To learn more about the John Maclean Foundation, log on to the Foundation website at www.jmf.com.au.

The John Maclean Foundation is a registered charity. Donations may be made through the website via a secure online transaction, or send a cheque or money order to:

The John Maclean Foundation
PO Box 6032
NORTH SYDNEY NSW 2060
AUSTRALIA

JOHN MACLEAN
FOUNDATION

INDEX

First published in 2005 by Pier 9, an imprint of Murdoch Books Australia Pty Limited
Reprinted 2005

Murdoch Books Australia
Pier 8/9
23 Hickson Road
Millers Point NSW 2000
Phone: +61 (0)2 8220 2000
Fax: +61 (0)2 8220 2558

Murdoch Books UK Limited
Erico House, 6th Floor North
93–99 Upper Richmond Road
Putney, London SW15 2TG
Phone: +44 (0) 20 8785 5995
Fax: + 44 (0) 20 8785 5985

www.murdochbooks.com.au

Chief Executive: Juliet Rogers
Publisher: Kay Scarlett

Commissioning Editor: Hazel Flynn
Design Manager: Vivien Valk
Concept and Design: Lauren Camilleri
Project Manager: Janine Flew
Editor: Anouska Jones
Production Manager: Megan Alsop
Cover and Front Flap Photographs: Lisa Saad

National Library of Australia Cataloguing-in-Publication Data
Maclean, John, 1966- . Sucking the marrow out of life : the John Maclean story.
Includes index. ISBN 1 74045 670 X. 1. Maclean, John, 1966- . 2. Athletes - Australia -
       Biography. I. Connolly, Paul, 1968- . II. Title. 796.4257092

Printed by McPherson's Printing Group in 2005. PRINTED IN AUSTRALIA.